CHILDHOOD MEMORIES

CHILDHOOD MEMORIES

*In aid of Action Research
for the Crippled Child*

**Introduced by
Paddington Bear**

MICHAEL O'MARA BOOKS LIMITED

First published in Great Britain in 1989 by
Michael O'Mara Books
Lion Yard, 11–13 Tremadoc Road
London SW4 7NF
in association with
Action Research for the Crippled Child Vincent House, North Parade,
Horsham, Sussex RH12 2DA

A CIP catalogue record for this book is available from the British Library

ISBN 0-948397-79-9

Typeset by Florencetype Ltd, Kewstoke, Avon
Printed and bound in Great Britain by Mackays of Chatham Ltd

The anthology has been compiled by Patricia Yeowart
with grateful thanks to Geoffrey Yeowart, Meri Benham, Anna-Rose Crichton-Stuart
Prudence Cuming, Tessa Dahl, Rosemary David, Gillian Evans, Susan Ferguson,
Mem FitzPatrick, Candida Hurst-Brown, Nicholas and Lavinia Owen,
Joanna Seligman and many others.

The publishers would like to thank all the contributors
for their kind help in supplying 'childhood memories' for this anthology.
Copyright in the individual pieces and photographs rests with the contributors,
as well as those publishers listed below.
Catherine Cookson (page 34) – From *Our Kate*, reprinted
by permission of Macdonald and Co. Ltd; Peter Cushing (page 36) – From
Peter Cushing: An Autobiography, reprinted by permission of George Weidenfeld
& Nicolson Ltd; Roald Dahl (page 38) – From *Boy*, reprinted by
permission of Roald Dahl and Jonathan Cape Ltd; Dame Daphne du Maurier
(page 42) – From *Growing Pains*, reprinted by permission of Victor Gollancz Ltd;
Graham Greene (page 56) – From *A Sort of Life*, reprinted by
permission of Graham Greene and Laurence Pollinger Ltd; Bernard Levin
(page 80) – From *Enthusiasms*, reprinted by permission of Jonathan Cape Ltd;
Sir John Mills (page 92) – From *Up in the Clouds, Gentlemen Please*,
reprinted by permission of George Weidenfeld & Nicolson Ltd; V.S. Pritchett
(page 112) – From *A Cab at the Door*, reprinted by permission of Chatto & Windus
Ltd; Ned Sherrin (page 119) – From *A Small Thing like an
Earthquake*, reprinted by permission of George Weidenfeld & Nicolson Ltd;
Sir Brian Rix (page 113) – From *My Farce from my Elbow*, reprinted by
permission of Martin, Secker & Warburg; Chris Tarrant (page 125) – From *Ken's
Furry Friends*, reprinted by permission of Macmillan Publishers Ltd;
Norman Thelwell (page 127) – From *Wrestling with a Pencil*,
reprinted by permission of Methuen London; Terry Wogan (page 143)
– From *Wogan's Ireland*, reprinted by permission
of Terry Wogan and Michael Joseph Ltd.

32 Windsor Gardens

I am delighted that so many famous people have contributed to this book of childhood ~~memem~~ories - espeshially as Action Research is such a good cawse.

I was asked to write about my own childhood, but Bears don't have one - they only have Cubhood.

Anyway, so much has happened to me since I came to England that I have forgotten most of my memories.

Mrs. Bird thinks they will come back to me when I am older, but the publishers don't think they can wait that long!

PADINGTON

Lord Aberconway
PRESIDENT EMERITUS OF THE ROYAL HORTICULTURAL SOCIETY

One of my godparents was a distinguished gardener, Ellen Willmott. I wrote to thank her for a birthday or Christmas present when I was six years old, in 1919, and after saying the usual things about how kind of her it was and how the present was just what I wanted, I must have sucked my pen and wondered how I could get onto the obligatory second page to this ghastly old bitch or whatever small children do think of their godmothers, and I wrote that our head gardener at Bodnant had died and my father was looking for another one. She wrote to my father asking if this was true, and if so, he should not fail to consider Mr Frederick Puddle. My father considered and appointed Mr Puddle, who in due course was succeeded by his son Charles, who again in due course was succeeded by his son Martin, who is now, after sixty-nine years, our third generation head gardener. And he has two young sons.

Lady Anson
CHAIRMAN OF THE HOUSING ASSOCIATION OF DISTRICT COUNCILS

As a child I lived in Somerset in the middle of a cider orchard full of wasps. I still remember Somerset wasps with a special sort of horror, and they always seemed worse on farms, but when we visited my uncle's farm I forgot about wasps while listening to his account of his most recent adventure.

Uncle Mortimer (and that really was his name) lived a constant life of adventure. My brother and I arrived one day not long before the first Christmas after the Second World War and were enlisted to help him set a trap. The trap was for chicken thieves who were busy that year as meat was still rationed and Black Market prices for Christmas dinners were high. Uncle Mortimer had always seemed an innocent farmer and had never been called up into the army as he was doing work of national importance. He told us now that in reality he had been in some sort of secret army ready if the Germans invaded Somerset, and he had unearthed some of his secret hoard of explosives. To children who had had six years of no Guy Fawkes and fireworks it was all very exciting.

Under his command we taped and fixed the packages we were given around the chicken run. Uncle Mortimer fitted a beam of wood by the hen house and linked that to a charge by the hen run gate so that if the gate was opened (in spite of a padlock) the charge would activate the log and hurtle it knee high across the hen run. We children had to go home early as we had seven miles to bicycle. We telephoned Uncle Mortimer next day but nothing had happened.

Then, the following morning at 6 o'clock we were woken by a telephone call. Uncle Mortimer was jubilant. 'They'll never be back again for my chickens' he boomed down the telephone wire. 'I woke at the explosion two hours ago and went to investigate. No one about but blood everywhere. Only trouble, we put in too much charge and the whole hen house is lying some yards from its foundations, and my damned chickens are all alive but are now naked of feathers.'

Jeffrey Archer

AUTHOR

I think the most frightening childhood memory of my life was a journey from Weston-super-Mare in Somerset to Leeds in Yorkshire. The purpose of the journey was to visit an aunt and uncle who were schoolteachers in North Allerton and as I had never travelled beyond Bristol or Bridgwater I looked forward to the day with much anticipation and relish. My grandmother was one of those early drivers who had not required a driving licence and had she ever taken the test she would have undoubtedly frightened the examiner out of his wits.

We left Weston-super-Mare early in the morning in a large green Morris Oxford car. My grandmother drove, my grand-father and mother were in the back while I had the honour of sitting in the front, decades before anyone had thought of seat belts. My grandmother, like myself, rarely travelled beyond the environs of Weston-super-Mare and for her the roundabout was a new-fangled invention which she had not encountered before. We discovered the first one some seven miles outside my home town. She happily drove straight across the middle of it and carried on in a northerly direction. We encountered twenty-three such obstacles set unnecessarily in our progress on our route between Weston-super-Mare and Leeds and my grand-mother crossed all of them in a manner which would have pleased Hannibal.

On arrival in Leeds my grandfather who had learned several years before not to speak, my mother who was not listened to when she did and I, who did not murmur a word, all breathed more than a sigh of relief when we eventually arrived at my uncle's front door in one piece. Once safely on the premises, I ventured the innocent question of my grandmother 'surely one should go around roundabouts and not across them?' to which she replied with British certainty, 'certainly not. What you must understand, young man, is that they will never catch on,' showing a degree of logic with which I am quite unable to find fault. We returned home by train.

Dr Mary Archer

SCIENTIST

I think I've always wanted to know what makes things tick. When I was about six, my father asked me what I wanted to be when I grew up, and my reply was 'I want to be an expert'. Exactly what I wanted to be an expert at wasn't clear to me until I was about ten. That's when I was first introduced to science, in a room at the top of my preparatory school that was half a laboratory and half a natural history museum. It was called the Discovery Room. In it there were wonderful things – a large crystal of quartz, small mammals pickled in bottles, a large brown-coloured globe and trays of germinating seeds. All this was much more fun than needlework and French, so much so that it set me on the path to becoming a scientist. In fact, the urge to experiment led to the only occasion on which I recall my father spanking me. I wanted to see if earthworms could untie themselves, so I seized an innocent worm and tied it into a knot. I don't recall what kind of knot it was, and certainly no knot I've tied since has shown any great inclination to stay fast. But that worm was stuck, and when my father came upon me and it, I was roundly scolded for my thoughtlessness, spanked and sent to bed early. To this day I cannot remember what happened to the unfortunate worm.

Paddy Ashdown MP

LEADER OF THE SOCIAL AND LIBERAL DEMOCRATS

I was brought up in India. My father was famous among his friends for having outlandish pets and I recall, for instance, a scaly ant eater which used to come in to our wooden bungalow quite frequently while we were having meals. It was a wonderful animal and used its long snout to 'hoover' the skirting boards for termites.

However, my favourite among the many animals my father had was a monkey. Though slightly older than me, it was about the same size and until my brother was old enough to play with, we were close companions! What made the monkey a particularly useful ally was that we seemed to take it in turns to be mischievous and, therefore, he would get beaten one day while I would get beaten the next.

On one occasion (I cannot remember for what) my father smacked the monkey harder than usual. Intelligent animal that it was, it scampered across to a low table on which my mother kept their only unbroken wedding present, a Wedgwood vase (one of the blue ones with Greek gods going round the side). Both the monkey and I knew that this was my mother's most precious possession, as it was brought out on all special occasions.

The monkey picked the vase up and scampered out of the front door and down the path which lead to our front gate, with both my parents in hot pursuit. It scrambled up a mango tree by the front gate and, sitting at the top, held the vase out and, after a delicious moment of suspense dropped it. Just as the vase passed its feet, its foot shot out and caught it. It did this a considerable number of times, with my parents quite frantic at the bottom of the tree, waiting to catch the vase! Having amused itself for ten minutes, the monkey descended the tree, laid the vase on the ground and walked away. To my chagrin, it was never beaten again.

Since then I have had a healthy respect for monkeys and always return to the monkey house whenever I visit a zoo in order to pay my respects.

The Duke of Atholl
CHAIRMAN OF WESTMINSTER PRESS AND CHAIRMAN OF RNLI

My cousin and I shared a French governess, whom we found enormously tiresome. One day she was determined we should play a game which she called 'La Flèche', whereby you followed arrows all over the garden. She was fairly new and did not know the garden, and when it came to her turn to follow the arrows, we pointed them at the raspberry cage, hid behind a bush, and when she had gone in, shut the gate (which could not be opened from the inside). All was well until tea-time, when her absence was noticed and enquiries made – retribution followed. But much to our joy she left soon afterwards.

The Rev. W.V. Awdry
AUTHOR AND CREATOR OF 'THOMAS THE TANK ENGINE'

My home, until the age of six, was at Ampfield Vicarage between Winchester and Romsey in Hampshire. An afternoon walk was a regular part of my upbringing as a small boy. Mother usually took me out, but on some days, Wednesdays I think, when she had a Mothers' Union or similar meeting, Father took me instead. I remember nothing of my walks with Mother, but Father's were quite different. We always went the same way, but always they were fun.

There were three delights which never palled. First a visit to the blacksmith's workshop. It was fascinating to watch him at work, shaping the red hot iron with such seemingly effortless hammer blows into a perfect horseshoe, the 'hoosh' with clouds of steam as it was quenched in cold water and the patient way the horse didn't seem to mind when it was nailed on to its hoof. Naturally I got a bit grubby here, but Father never seemed to mind as Mother would, for what we did next would soon take care of that!

Opposite the blacksmith's workshop a lane turned off the Romsey road. This was an exciting place for a small boy too. The lane twisted away on a gentle downward slope. Flowing alongside it was a sizeable stream fed by the overflow from a cattle-trough in a nearby field. This lane-side stream, as I remember it, was always fast flowing, and the exciting thing about it was not only the rate at which it flowed, but also that as the lane twisted, so it changed course from one side of the lane to the other flowing through tunnels underneath the road. It was tremendous fun to launch paper boats, of which Father usually had a supply, and scamper along beside them with a stick to free them from obstacles on their voyage, and to watch them dive into the tunnels and wait anxiously for them to emerge. In the end I seem to remember that we found bits of stick preferable to paper boats. Paper boats soon got water-logged and sank, while carefully chosen sticks withstood the buffetting of the stream and were more likely to slip through the tunnels and emerge bravely on the other side. Father would roll up my sleeves, and hanging on to me as best he could, let me chase along with my 'boats'. Inevitably, I sometimes fell in and play ended, but Father turned that into fun too. He would whisk me back and we crept in by the back door and he often managed to get me clean and into dry clothes before we told Mother anything about it!

Another delight lay further along that lane, a delight that only Father could give. He sometimes had special information from railwaymen friends that something interesting was happening. It might be a new locomotive fresh from Eastleigh Works on running trials, or a special train for Royalty or a visiting VIP, or even if the local platelayers gang were working on the Baddesley stretch. We would start out in good time and ignoring both blacksmith and stream, would follow the lane till we came to a railway bridge. A gate on the right opened into a field through which the railway embankment ran. We would scramble up and walk along the trackside until, over the bridge, the track base widened and we could stand further back and wait for whatever was to come. A thrilling experience for a small boy to hear first the humming of the rails made by the approaching train and as it came closer and swept by to feel the pleasurable excitement and vibration of its passing. If the gangers were at work we would stay and watch them, Father explaining to me what they were doing and why. No-one ever turned us away. They were all Father's parishioners and knew him to be more knowledgeable than most in railway affairs. If, as often happened, it came on to rain we would adjourn to their lineside hut built of old sleepers where they made us very welcome. I thought the hut marvellous; Mother would have thought it

11

dirty, smelly and smoky – but to me it had an almost fairytale air about it. I would listen to Father and the men talking about their railway, their work and their pride in both. At the age of four or five I cannot have understood much of it; but, young as I was, I must have absorbed something of the atmosphere which has stayed with me throughout life.

The Rt. Hon. Kenneth Baker MP

SECRETARY OF STATE FOR EDUCATION

I was at school in Southport, during the Second World War, and the memories of those years are still very vivid. One thing that I do remember very clearly was the very long summer evenings. We had double Summer Time which meant it was light well up to ten or eleven o'clock. I well remember those long and sunny evenings.

We lived right alongside the beach. There was a golf course very close but during the war it had ceased being played on. It was just growing grass, which was cut and turned into hay by a farmer. I remember what fun it was to go along in the evening and climb on the haystacks. In those days they made rather old-fashioned haystacks which you see in old paintings – square, with pointed roofs like cottages. Sliding down them was tremendous fun. But after a time you wore away the stack and it became one huge mass of hay and so these hay-climbing expeditions were rather perilous because the farmer would try to catch you.

One evening my sister was caught on the top of the haystack when the farmer turned up. We had to try and distract him into chasing us as she got down. This simple strategy worked – but we had to help repair the haystack.

Richard Baker

BROADCASTER

If you are of an imaginative turn of mind as a child, it can lead you into dreadful trouble, and I relate the following story as an awful warning.

We lived some little distance from the school I attended in north London from the age of eight to eleven, and as those were the days before most families had a car, I walked in both directions. On the way there, I called for a couple of other boys whose houses lay on the route, and together we proceeded on our way. Little did they know that I was the veteran of many a trip down the Thames to Margate on the paddle steamer *Crested Eagle* and, in imagination, on these walks to school, I was the captain of the *Crested Eagle* calling at various piers on the way down river to pick up more passengers.

The walk was long and often rather boring, and after a time even this beguiling fantasy must have palled, for on the way home one day, before allowing my 'passengers' to alight at their respective ports of call, I decided to tell a story. Just to pass the time, you understand. It was a dramatic tale and I was gratified by the rapt attention with which it was received.

Our house had been broken into by armed robbers. All my mother's valuable jewels (she had only a single string of Woolworth's pearls) had been stolen. I had returned home from playing in the park and discovered them redhanded. Fearlessly I had chased them from the house but they got away, and my poor mother was distraught at the loss of her valuable possessions. One after another my friends left me, with reluctance, and I went on my way home alone.

While I was eating tea in the kitchen the front door bell rang. My mother answered it and through the kitchen door I heard the ensuing conversation. 'Oh, Mrs Baker' said the visitor, 'Bob has just told me about your terrible robbery. All your jewels . . . my dear!' My mother was totally at a loss. 'What robbery?' she asked. 'What jewels?'

'You mean to say that what your Richard told my Bob was NOT TRUE?' 'Well, if he told him that, I'm afraid it wasn't,' said my mother who was both baffled and distressed. 'Then I shall never, ever allow Bob to speak to him again,' said Bob's mother. 'Your Richard is a dreadful liar. And I shall tell all the other mothers in the road about him.'

For a long while after that, my walks to school and back seemed even longer. The *Crested Eagle* had no calls to make, either coming or going. But I learned a lesson. If you must tell stories, try not to make them too interesting.

Dame Josephine Barnes

GYNAECOLOGIST

My earliest memories go back to the First World War. I was the eldest of five children and my brother was born when I was less than eighteen months old. So my earliest memories are of walking – walking to church and always walking beside the prams which contained my various siblings.

Naturally my memories of that war are now incomplete. We lived in Exeter and three times a year we made our pilgrimage to our grandmother who lived in York. Those train journeys seemed endless and we counted every station along the way. I did see a German zeppelin and was once taken to the cellar when an air raid was threatened. My father as an Army chaplain came and went. I remember the awful casualty lists and the reference that so and so had been killed. I do remember the shell which hit Scarborough and killed the Sitwells' housemaid.

When that war ended I walked beside the pram in Exeter High Street waving a Union Jack with little idea what it was about. The centre of Exeter I knew then was largely destroyed in the Second World War. VE day is a vivid memory, the lights going up and London crowded with cheering hysterical crowds. VJ day was much quieter. I went with a friend to the New Theatre in London. I cannot remember what we saw but I do remember that Winston Churchill with his wife and daughter Mary were there, and though he was now in opposition they were cheered to the roof.

Ian Beer

HEADMASTER OF HARROW SCHOOL

It was October 1939. We lived in south London and at the age of eight I had just heard war declared on the radio, listened to the first of many air-raid sirens and began to prepare myself for the invasion which seemed to be not far off. Everyone was busy. Sandbags, brown paper strips to be stuck on all the windows, black curtains and the daily testing of gas masks became the new life which war had somehow created for me. I was summoned by my father and informed that I had an important task to do as I

14

had been appointed to be in charge of the issue of ear-plugs for the whole of our avenue! I was thrilled to be of use.

I was given the tools of my new trade and set off, an important official, to fulfill my new role. At each house I knocked on the door, or rang the bell, asked to speak to the householder and requested to know the number of people who lived there. I then counted out the appropriate number of pieces of string from one box I carried round my neck, and twice the number of small, brown rubbery ear-plugs from my other box. It was then my task to show how the string could be tied around the neck of each ear-plug and the string worn round the neck like a chain bearing its owner's glasses. Forever more I could see all our friends at the alert ready to insert their ear-plugs the moment the bombs came. I suppose it was my first taste of responsibility. I never wore my ear-plugs despite all those bombs in the coming years; I often wonder what became of the hundreds this tiny official issued for I cannot recall ever seeing anyone wearing them.

Lynda Bellingham

ACTRESS

As a child of nearly eleven I dreamed of owning a pony. During this year leading to my eleventh birthday I went to Italy on holiday with my parents and we visited Rome. Among the sights was the famous Trevi fountain. I threw in my coin and asked for a pony.

The nearest I had got to owning one was riding a pony in the stables down the road. She was called Tiddliwinks. How I loved her! I used to go down every day to see her and ride her. My fantasy was that on my eleventh birthday Dad would say 'Look out of the window, Lynda,' and I would see Tiddliwinks in the paddock. Well, having wished with all my heart in Rome, my eleventh birthday arrived, and believe it or not my Father whispered the immortal words – I could not believe he had actually said go and look or that I would see what I had dreamed of time after time in the last few months. But Tiddliwinks was there alright – all saddled up and ready to go.

I ran down and out into the paddock, got on, and, would you believe it, she bucked me off. It was very undignified and not the end I had hoped for – not like the films, but the end was happy eventually and we became firm friends.

Rachel Billington

NOVELIST, PLAYWRIGHT AND CRITIC

He had lustrous black eyes, thick curly hair, and a walk that turned into a swagger. He stood in the yard and all us stable girls, unpaid muckers-out, tack cleaners and horse-lovers, stared. He stared back. Then he swaggered a step or two towards us and said, with a voice too baritone for one so young 'Hood Monnin'. This was Ernest, Ernesto in his native Seville, who became hero for one whole summer of the Birchgrove Riding School.

He had few rivals: although there was Paul. Paul could cross his long legs and rest them on the handlebars of his bicycle. But his skin was pale and his hair lank and in general he had the look of vitamin deficiency common in East Sussex, class of 1958, particularly when contrasted with a product of sunny skies and oranges growing on trees. Also, in Ernest's case, the confidence given by an adoring Latin mother and doting sisters.

For Ernest was conceited. He strode among us girls like a pasha and we waited humbly to be chosen. Why he chose me is uncertain. It could have been my seat – on horseback that is: 'she has a neat little seat' said my end of summer riding school report. It could have been my hands light on the reins . . . But in fact I suspect it was merely my long brown plaits and my sunburned skin which reminded him of home. His ardour, of course, was irresistible. 'I hgluff voo, Rachelle,' he said not once but often. My affections, not without guilt, were transferred from a fourteen-hand chestnut gelding. I did worry, however, about the appropriate response to his passion. Luckily, I soon recognized that his was a one-person drama. 'I hgluff you!' accompanied by fulsome hand gestures, gave him so much pleasure that he was too dazzled to notice what I might be saying, doing or feeling. I was a love object – which perfectly suited my thirteen-year-old's reticence.

Our romance was limited not only by Ernest's nature but by its equine setting. We were often on horseback and when we were not I was earning my rides by removing horse dung from one area of the stable yard to another. Since Ernest was not a confident *caballero* and had not been brought up to consider manual labour either duty or fun, his protestations were saved for the momentary tranquility of late afternoons. 'I weel

Below left: The Begum Aga Khan as a baby
with her father in India
Right: Paddy Ashdown at prep school
Below right: Jeffrey Archer aged eleven

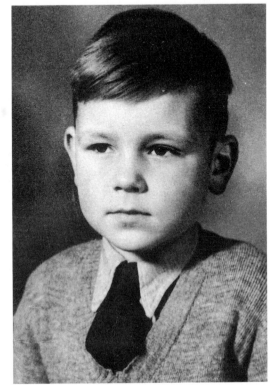

Below: Katie Boyle as a young girl
Right: The Rev. W.V. Awdry as a little boy
Far below: The Rt. Hon. Kenneth Baker MP in an Empire Day parade (second boy from left)

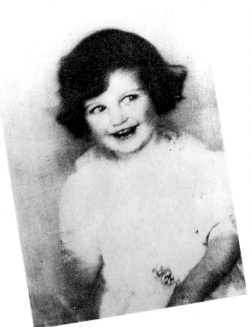

Left: Gyles Brandreth aged eleven
Below: Michael Buerk aged six
Far below: Jilly Cooper aged eleven with her pony Willow

Above: Peter Cushing aged two
Right: Sir Robin Day aged five
Below: Johnny Dumfries at the wheel of his
cousin's racing car

remaimba yoo eternal.' Separating each of my fingers, he kissed them one by one.

Naturally, I kept such glorious passion hidden from my family. Four older brothers and sisters and three younger could be counted on to disdain, disbelieve or ridicule. I was a rosy-cheeked schoolgirl and in their view, unable to inspire 'The eternal'. When Ernest returned to Spain I wandered soulfully among our rhododendrons even though my mourning had an air of unreality. Even when I sat on the swing hung among disconsolate pine trees proper misery failed to surface. Ernest had taken his love with him.

Or so I thought. The first package arrived at breakfast time. Since it was not my birthday nor Christmas, everyone's attention was rivetted as I untied knot after knot, unwrapped layer after layer of paper and revealed in a box at the centre – a ring. 'Rachel's been sent a ring!' shrieked my brothers and sisters. 'From a boy in Spain. And the ring's squashed,' observed a sharp-eyed brother. He was right. Despite all the wrapping, the ring was as squashed as if an elephant had sat on it, and when I held it up, the central stone popped out and fell into my cereal. How could Ernest put me through such embarrassment?

This was only the start. Next to arrive were Toledo-ware earrings with a faulty clasp. Then there was a glass necklace in five pieces, a loving cup in ten pieces and a bracelet in twenty-three pieces. After a short pause in which I prayed daily that the value of the *peseta* should halve, a particularly large parcel disgorged a Spanish doll complete with mantilla and castanets but whose eyes had fallen to the back of her head. 'Rachelle's admirer has such lovely taste but such bad luck with the Post Office!' gloated my brothers and sisters. Breakfast had never been such fun.

Even worse, the parcels were accompanied by loving notes. Mispronounced endearments, so charming in the flesh, were truly idiotic on paper. 'I is strocking yoo check' needed the touch of a slim brown hand. 'You fingys are sweater than biscits' made slightly more sense than 'You lips are red as cherrio.' The notes were found, of course, and caused near ecstacy among my insensitive siblings. In the end I had no choice. 'I HATE Ernest!' I shouted. By now it was St Valentine's day and I had just received a pin cushion shaped like a heart. One of the pins had torn through the satin so that sawdust dripped out like tears. Taking firm strides, I threw Ernest's heart into the dustbin.

The Rt. Hon. The Lord Birkett

FILM-MAKER AND ARTS ADMINISTRATOR

RIGHT!
When I was one, when I was one
I knew at once, It had begun.
When I was two, when I was two
I weighed it up. I thought it through.
When I was three, when I was three
I knew the world was made for me.
When I was four, when I was four
I'd conquered half the world and more.
When I was five, when I was five
A few more senses came alive.
When I was six, when I was six
Nothing was left I couldn't fix.
When I was seven, when I was seven
I knew the route-map straight from heaven.
When I was eight, when I was eight
I'd done it all. I couldn't wait . . .
And now I'm nearly fifty-nine
I'm not convinced the world is mine.
So hard to see, the whole design,
Is it, I wonder, all divine?
Still and all, no use to pine,
Mustn't whimper, mustn't whine.
Stiffen the shoulders, brace the spine,
Pour another glass of wine.
It's clear, so clear, it's crystalline,
That I was right. In '29!

Michael Bond

AUTHOR AND CREATOR OF 'PADDINGTON BEAR'

I was born in Newbury, England, on 13 January 1926. The event went unreported in *The Times* of London, which was more concerned with matters like the theft of a motor car and its contents, the adverse trade balance (nothing changes!), and something they called 'weather probabilities'.

I weighed over eleven pounds at birth and my mother used to stand me in bowls of Tidman's Sea Salt to stop me going bandy when I started to walk. It must have done the trick because in early photographs I look perfectly normal.

Mother was a great believer in old-fashioned remedies for aches and pains, and looking back she was probably right; at least they were all tried and tested and none of them had any side effects. Calves' Foot Jelly cured most things, a nightly spoonful of Virol built me up during the week, and on Friday night a dose of California Syrup of Figs prepared me for Sunday lunch and ensured a constipation-free start to the following week.

She always saw things in black and white; there were never any shades of grey in her life. If she went out after dark, which rarely happened, it was always 'pitch black' outside. Hot drinks, if they were left too long, became 'stone cold'. When it rained, it invariably rained 'cats and dogs', and if a light was accidentally left on it had always been left 'full on'.

Life was very tranquil in those pre-war days. Television hadn't been invented, so people had to devise their own entertainment. I don't think I ever went to bed without a story. The word 'radio' still often meant a crystal set, and if you entered a room and saw someone wearing headphones you had to be very careful how you closed the door in case the 'cat's whisker' became detached at a critical moment in the programme.

Practically everything was delivered to the house; freshly baked bread arrived by horse-drawn van, vegetables by horse and cart, milk came in churns on a hand cart and it was always the high spot of the day to be allowed to take a jug into the street so that a pint could be poured from a copper and brass measure. There were no refrigerators, so in the summer it went off very quickly. For the same reason pork was only eaten when there was an *R* in the month. Strawberries arrived in time for Ascot Week and were a great treat. They stayed for Wimbledon, then disappeared again. There was no question of their being available at any other time of the year, but we enjoyed them much more because of that and I'm sure they tasted nicer.

Street games came and went in strict rotation. Hoops made of iron or wood came out as if by magic on a certain day; tops appeared on another. Roller skates had their place in the calendar. Mine always came from Woolworths and cost sixpence each part – two parts to a skate. They seldom lasted a season and usually ended up sagging in the middle where the two halves joined. Conkers, baked in the oven and threaded onto a string, heralded the approach of winter and we looked forward to Sunday afternoons when the sound of a handbell meant the Muffin Man was making his rounds.

Memory plays strange tricks, but the seasons also seemed more clearly defined. The winters were colder. There was always snow, and ponds froze over, so there was skating. By contrast the summers were long and hot. I used to play endless games of cricket with my father in the local park. He did all the bowling and running for the ball, while I batted. He was a very kind and patient man who knew that the most important thing you can give a child is your time; a belief he must have been sorely tempted to forgo after a hard day at the office when I stood, bat in hand, breathing down the back of his neck while he tried to eat his 'high tea'. How he must have prayed for rain to stop play.

Holidays were taken at Sandown, on the Isle of Wight. Armed with suitcases and buckets and spades we would set off by steam train to Portsmouth Harbour in carriages decorated with sepia photographs and maps of Southern England. An added excitement was catching the ferry across to the island. In those days 'going to the Island' was the equivalent of going abroad – a possibility which wouldn't have occurred to my parents in their wildest dreams, even if they had been able to afford it. Mother didn't really hold with such things, although I'm sure my father would have been game for he had served in France in the First War.

On the other hand, I don't remember him ever making any concession to being on the beach other than taking his shoes and socks off and rolling up the bottoms of his flannel trousers in case the tide came in. In all the holiday photographs still in my possession he is wearing a jacket and tie, often a waistcoat too, and smoking the inevitable pipe. More often than not he kept his hat on as well. Being a very polite man he liked to have something to raise when he met anyone he knew and he always felt lost without it. We used to stay at a 'guest house' run by a Mr and Mrs Gate, who expected their guests to be out all day whatever the weather. It was situated on top of the cliffs overlooking the bay, and my father would give me a piggyback up the long path home every evening.

They were happy days, and looking back I realize my parents must have gone without a lot in order to bring me up in what mother would have called 'the right way'. At the time I took it all very much for granted. My only regret is that it is too late now to say 'thank you'.

When I came to write the Paddington books I drew heavily on my childhood memories. Mr and Mrs Brown are very like my parents, although I doubt if they would have recognized themselves – people rarely do. Paddington exists in a very contemporary world and he wouldn't be at all taken aback by the sight of a fax machine or the thought of going to the moon, but when he goes on family expeditions or has a day out with his friend, Mr Gruber, it is usually a journey back in time as well.

His outings take him into another world; a world as I remember it, with a different set of values.

When Paddington goes to the seaside it is a seaside with Punch and Judy shows and sticks of rock with the name of the town going all the way through, and donkey rides and the excitement of going on the pier with its strange machines – 'What the Butler Saw' (not a lot as I remember it, but then I didn't really know what he was looking for!), and a contraption which, on payment of a penny, enabled you to punch out your name and address on a strip of aluminium – and band concerts, and the thrill of looking at the sea through gaps in the boards, and paddle steamers leaving for the mainland.

On the other hand, I doubt very much if Mr Brown would ever give Paddington a piggy-back home at the end of the day, and I can't say I blame him. There's a limit to most things, even for bears.

Roy Boulting

FILM PRODUCER, DIRECTOR AND WRITER

I have to tell you that there's something very odd about twins. And, of course, when you come to think about it, there has to be. Over the years, I've done a deal of thinking on the subject: I like to call it, research. And, in the process of asking myself 'how and why' twins are so strange, odd, removed from the main stream of ordinary mortals, I have become, if not obsessed, certainly fascinated. Let me explain.

Oh, by the way – I'll not be giving much of a mention to the two-cell, two fertilized ovary jobs in all of this. In my view, they don't truly belong to the genus; and, again, because as 'twins', I don't really rate 'em. They're fakes! Period. After all, theirs is nothing more than a simple multiplication: two human embryos instead of one. They may feed from the same source, but they live quite separate lives in the womb from day one to month nine. After which, fully formed, they find themselves turfed out, born on the same day, and become 'pretenders to Twindom'. But, if still interested, you persist in asking, 'Nevertheless, how come, two?', I'll throw you a provisional hypothesis before moving on to the exciting bit: it could be a Father, fully charged, panting to get to the job of producing a family over and done with as quickly as possible; alternatively, a Mother possessed of extraordinary fecundity; or, both. But, as I say – they may be termed 'Twins' – but not in my book!

For me, the real McCoy, the 100 per cent genuine, copperbottomed duality is the product of a much rarer, mysterious and special process. To begin with, conception starts with only one egg being fertilized. Up to that point, modest, reserved – British. Ah, but what follows? At a quite arbitrary moment in gestation, for heaven knows what reason, the fertilized ovary decides to divide, break into two parts and emerge, in due course, as – Identical Twins! – same colour eyes, same colour hair and skin, same shaped bones and limbs and parts – each Babe a mirror image of the other – identical! Not so, the 'pretenders'. Beyond a mere family likeness, probably as dissimilar as chalk and cheese. 'Okay', I hear you exclaim. 'So these are the *real* twins. But in what way are they so odd, so special?' At this moment, perhaps, I should disclose a special interest: I am a twin myself. What is more, despite all the clucking of old wives – 'Then *you* don't have to worry, do you? Twins always skip a generation' – I've even managed to sire a pair, myself. Rupert and Edmund. Splendid fellows.

Born a twin, throughout childhood you remain largely innocent, unaware of your oddness, although grown-ups – parents, relatives and benevolent-looking old ladies – sprinkle warning clues in your path a-plenty. John and I were raised in a nursery with a nanny on whose capacious, white starched, aproncovered bosom we would throw our tears and troubles. It was when she took us out on afternoon walks that we first became conscious of our 'apartness'. With Guy, our younger brother, propped up in the pram, we were a fair target for the inquisitive: 'Oh, do forgive us, Nanny! They *must* be twins, surely?' Not the most brilliant piece of deduction, seeing that we looked alike, were dressed alike, had our hair cut alike, were both blushing, squirming, hopping from one foot to the other in embarrassment alike; and hating Guy – an infinitely prettier child – for being totally disregarded and unremarked. And, all the time, Nanny standing there, proud and preening.

Later, away at school, came other forms of victimization. As neither masters, nor prefects, could ever distinguish between Boulting Major and Boulting Minor (me!), when uncertainty arose as to which one had offended, we both of us suffered a beating to make certain that justice had been done! With like iniquities, were our youthful, early adolescent years, studded.

Gyles Brandreth

**AUTHOR, BROADCASTER AND FOUNDER OF THE
NATIONAL TEDDY BEAR MUSEUM**

In 1957 I was nine years old and quite small. General Charles de Gaulle was President of France at the time, rather older than me and certainly a great deal taller. In the summer of that year we were due to meet. I don't know if the General was keenly anticipating the encounter, but rest assured I was. Not since Stanley met Livingstone had there been a handshake of such moment. The reason for this epic Anglo-French get-together was simply that General de Gaulle was on a State Visit to the United Kingdom and I happened to be a pupil at the French School in London. It had been decided that the President would find time between lunch at Buckingham Palace and supper at 10 Downing Street for tea at the Lycée Français de Londres where a small band of pupils was to be presented to him. For weeks we were carefully drilled in anticipation of the great day. We learned all seven verses of the French National Anthem (oui, sept!) and time and again we rehearsed the firm handshake that was to be accompanied by a smart bob of the head.

At long last the day was upon us and at the given hour I and half a dozen other representatives of Anglo-French youth were lined up outside the Lycée waiting for the presidential limousine. Absolutely on schedule the gigantic General stepped from his car, was greeted by our Headmaster and led towards the line where we boys and girls were waiting. I was fourth to be presented. President de Gaulle shook the hand of the first pupil. He then shook the hand of the second pupil. He then shook the hand of the third pupil and even exchanged a few words with him. He then shook the hand of the fifth pupil. And then the sixth. And then the seventh. And then the eighth. And then he was away into the building and out of my life. I knew I was small, but I had never felt that small before.

Of course, I consoled myself with the thought that the slight wasn't deliberate, that the great man was so tall that he simply didn't notice this shrimp in the line-up. And then exactly ten years later, when I was an undergraduate at Oxford, I was invited to have tea with Harold Macmillan. Knowing that Supermac and de Gaulle had been acquaintances if not quite bosom buddies, I thought that my anecdote about my failed encounter with Le Général would amuse the former Prime Minister. When I arrived at the tea party I found that Mr Macmillan was already there and seated by the fire, but dozing gently. My hosts said they felt it would be a shame to disturb him. I waited for two hours for the great man to wake up. I enjoyed two toasted tea-cakes and several sandwiches, but I'm afraid I did not enjoy any small talk with Harold Macmillan. He slept throughout our encounter and after two hours when I slipped away I think he was even more profoundly asleep than when I arrived. I realized then that obviously he and de Gaulle had been in it together.

Raymond Briggs
WRITER AND ILLUSTRATOR

When I was about ten I had a craze for spoonerisms. Two friends and I would talk to one another in spoonerisms all the time. It became a speech habit and went on for *weveral seeks*. I think *Hommy Tandley* and ITMA may have had something to do with it. It is a *hilly sabit* which persists even to this day. It afflicts me at *stroments of mess* and at this age must indicate a *broftening of the sain*. However, to return to 1944.

My parents had some posh people to tea one day, so Mum put on her best frock with the padded shoulders, Dad put on a shiny

24

crimson tie and a home-knitted cardigan and I was scrubbed up and Brylcreemed till I shone all over.

We then sat round the starched white tablecloth, politely passing plates and clearing our throats. The posh people were so posh they actually put the dollop of jam on their plates instead of on the bread! I was amazed. Even then they didn't spread it. They put a clot of jam from the dollop onto their bread then bit this piece out of the slice. I quickly realized they got more jam that way and bore it in mind.

All was going quite well: Mum was relapsing into her normal accent and so far Dad, with his big hands, had not spilled anything or knocked anything over.

It was all going surprisingly well, but it was then I asked for a bit of sugar . . .

Sir Robin Butler KCB, CVO
SECRETARY FOR THE CABINET AND HEAD OF THE HOME CIVIL SERVICE

This is a letter (written as an exercise and not sent) to the Headmaster of Harrow School when I was thirteen.

Orley Farm School,
Harrow-on-the-Hill.

8 June

Dear Dr Moore,

I will be glad to accept the scholarship which you very kindly have granted me, and will be honoured to come to your fine school next term. As to my standard of work, you will doubtless have judged that by my exam papers. However, I would tell you that my favourite subject is maths, also with French, History, Geography, English, and Scripture close behind. I hate classics beyond all bounds, can't stand classical music, can't sing, and have no taste for the arts. I would warn you that I have a very fiery temper, and am positively dangerous when on the losing side. My favourite sports are cricket, rugger, and table tennis, but I hate gym. I hope you will find this interesting as my candid opinion of myself.

Yours,
R. Butler

Marti Caine

COMEDIENNE AND SINGER

From being a toddler I had a cat called Blackie who, much to his indignation, was forcibly clad in doll's clothes with his ears flattened under a woolly bonnet, front paws forced through the sleeves of the jacket and tail threaded through a strategically cut hole in the footed leggings. He looked very like an angry monkey.

To further his misery and my merriment, I would then strap him into my doll's pram, tuck him in neatly, then push him and the pram down the four front steps. The missile was brought to a sudden stop by a low brick wall. However, on a good day the mattress, covers and cat would continue the mystery tour and catapult – squawking – onto the lawn.

Miraculously the cat lived to see his eighteenth birthday, by cleverly avoiding me until I was a teenager.

Simon Callow

ACTOR

My mother was determined that my father's desertion of us was not going to cramp our lives, hers or mine. On one occasion, she popped off to Spain for six months leaving me in the highly capable care of my grandmothers; on another, she took a job as school secretary at a boarding school, with my education thrown in as a bonus, part, in fact, of her payment. The school, idyllically located at Goring-on-Thames, downstream from Reading, was intended for the children of rich foreigners whose eighteen-year-old sons were about to go to Oxford or Cambridge and needed to speak at least a modicum of English by the time they arrived there. For some reason all the boys were Spanish, and a team of Spaniards had been assembled, there in the Berkshire countryside, to teach them and feed them. The school was actually run, though, by a man who spoke no word of Spanish, who was in fact absurdly English: Roland Birch, tall, balding, middle-aged, displaying under his invariable khaki shorts, knobbly knees, a sort of elderly boy scout in appearance, but one who was never Prepared, and whose badges would have proved on examination, to be fraudulently acquired. I had little to do with him, and little, alas, to do with the 'boys', those Alvaros, Antonios and Franciscos, tall and black-haired, who seemed never to attend classes and to be always in pursuit of female flesh, the maid, the cook, or indeed, my mother.

The only female in the place who was safe from their frank lust was Roland Birch's mother, a woman of uncertain age, indeterminate shape and a rather vigorous growth of facial hair, whom I loved deeply. She was set the task of schooling me. I was a 'difficult' child, talkative, emotional and scattered, but I didn't seem to be a problem to her. Gathering me to her lap, she taught me to read. I seem to remember the moment, the very moment at which the hieroglyphs on the page suddenly spoke. I ran from the field in which the miracle occurred to find my mother. She received the news with tremendous gravity: 'Now you have the key with which you can open all the secrets of the world.' Later, I sat with Mrs Birch in her room, and again sitting on her lap, surrounded by her hairy warmth, I saw my first play. It was *Macbeth*: on the radio. We saw it together, and nothing, alas, that I have done or seen has ever been as powerful and terrible as what we saw in that room.

Brian Cant

CHILDREN'S TELEVISION PRESENTER

A sunny Sunday morning! I'm in the garden with my mother and father. From inside the house come the chimes of Big Ben striking eleven o'clock. My mother says 'He's on!' and they rush indoors and settle to listen to the radio. I wander in to hear a solemn voice saying '. . . and as we have received no such undertaking we are at war!' (Or similar words.)

The time – 11.00 a.m., Sunday 16 September 1939. I was six. We lived next door to my Uncle George and Auntie Amy. By 11.30 they were all in our garden discussing the 'digging of a trench'. Unhelpfully I suggested they should dig it half one side of the garden path and half the other (thinking of it as needing to be like a celery trench!). They, of course, were discussing an 'air-raid shelter'. That evening, the siren sounded and we were found sitting in a shack made out of old bits of plywood and 'two-by-one'. A clumsy vole could have demolished it!

Harry Carpenter

SPORTS COMMENTATOR

My mother, I think, liked the cinema. The Hollywood world of the 1930s was pure fantasy, a world of luxury homes, film stars dressed to the nines, an Astaire-Rogers world where the nice people behaved impeccably and the baddies got their just desserts. She did not care for gangster movies, but I did, so we went to those as well. My mother was quite selfless where I was concerned and we went to the pictures every Wednesday afternoon on my half-day off from school.

The Regal cinema at Beckenham in Kent was 100 yards from the bus-stop, which itself was conveniently placed in front of a toyshop. The window of the toyshop was required viewing for me when we came out of the pictures. I never wanted the bus to arrive too quickly.

One Wednesday, the week before my twelfth birthday, I looked in the toyshop window and saw something I wanted more than anything else in the world: a typewriter. Not a grown-up's typewriter, of course, but a model with a circular dial and rubber pimples. You pressed a pimple and the rubber impressed a letter on the paper. Then you wound the dial round to the next letter, pressed a pimple and another letter appeared on paper. I fancied myself as a story writer. I had seen the glamorous lives such people lived in my Wednesday trips to the cinema. The typewriter was essential if my life was to unfold as I now wanted it to. The typewriter had a price-tag affixed: five shillings.

Now, five shillings (25p) may not sound much today, but in the days when I was at school, the average wage was, I suppose, well under £5 a week. And five shillings for a child's birthday present was extravagance of a high order. Not that I realized it at the time. I pointed to the typewriter in the window. My mother saw the price-tag. I imagine she must have reeled back in shock. I said I would like the typewriter for my birthday. My mother tactfully expressed doubt that it could be done. We got on the bus and I knew – I just knew – that the typewriter would not be mine.

But there it was the following week when I woke up on my birthday. Somehow my mother had talked my father into springing the five-bob that would turn my birthday into a day such as I have all too seldom experienced since, a day of unalloyed joy and delight. I learned to turn that dial and press those pimples at an expert speed. I churned out page after page of childish rubbish.

I don't know what became of the typewriter. I imagine it went for scrap in the war. But I wound up as a journalist and I believe absolutely that the whole of my life was determined by that chance glance in the toyshop window after a trip to the pictures.

Jonathan Cecil

ACTOR

My most amusing childhood memory concerns my younger brother Hugh – now a don at Leeds University, then a most unpredictable boy of scarcely five; often lost in his imagination, now and again carried away in an exuberant fit of joy or rage.

My mother had taken him with her to Baker's, a depressing Oxford china shop, starkly lit and crammed with tasteless figurines. She was ordering plates from an overbearing female assistant with a blue rinse and severe spectacles. My brother, meanwhile, was running happily and harmlessly about, no doubt imagining himself to be a car or some exotic animal.

'Naughty little boy!' the assistant snapped. 'Naughty little boy! He shouldn't be allowed . . . Madam, please control him.'

In a trice, before my mother could say a word, my brother had planted himself – a tiny, furious figure – in front of the assistant.

'I'm very, very angry!' he said. 'When I'm grown up I'll box off your head!' Then crescendo, 'You're a HORRIBLE lady!'

The lady herself could only manage a tremulous 'OO-OOh!' in reply.

My mother, shaking with barely suppressed mirth, whisked my brother out of the shop and hurried home to tell me about the incident. This quite restored me as I lay in bed with seasonal 'flu and I remember asking for the story to be told over and over again to never-failing fits of laughter.

Bobby Charlton

FOOTBALL MANAGER

When I was twelve I got a job as a film runner after waiting for ages. It was the plum job for kids. Better than store deliveries or paper rounds. Let me explain the job. In Ashington North'd where I lived there were four cinemas, the Regal, Buffalo (Buff), Pavilion (Pivi) and the Wallaw, the last named after Walter Lawson the owner, who had been the last mine owner in the area until the nationalization of the mining industry. During the week all picture houses had different programmes but on Sundays the same two features were shown at all four, which meant a shuttle service of reels and this was done by kids like me speeding by bike round town at a great lick. If you were late for some reason (puncture or something interesting in a shop window) a baying crowd of irate filmgoers would greet your arrival with whistles and footstamping, but if you were early you could look through the small windows in the projection room and see Gene Kelly or Donald O'Connor dancing or Roy Rogers chasing cars on Trigger yodelling at the same time. What paradise for me; and they even paid four shillings (20p) but more importantly two *free* passes to all cinemas that week. No television in those days remember, so we were kings. Then one Sunday I was stopped by a policeman who said Mr Lawson was using child labour and we were to stop. As I had become hooked on films you can imagine I was gutted. I had loved it and didn't consider it work. Even now, when watching some film from the 1940s, I will remember a clip or two from those days but never the whole film. What memories. What pleasure.

Paul Coia

TELEVISION QUIZMASTER

Written as a child to give as a present to a friend.

> On Easter we get chocolate eggs
> Made by the faries
> On the paper duck's with long legs
> Or maybe pretty daisies

Inside your egg pretty sweets
Or maybe a nice thing
And you can here in the streets
Everybody starting to sing

Though Easter comes once a year
We all go to our bed
And nobody can here
For Easter is dead

Shirley Conran

AUTHOR

I have found early disasters to be quite useful in later life. At school as a twelve-year-old, I was the worst member of the gym team, and had to work hard to get into the team. We were taught two things by Miss Haydock, the St Paul's gym instructor: 1. Never give up. 2. What matters most is how you finish a movement, i.e. finish correctly and smoothly and completely.

Once at a gym display I ruined an intricate Busby-Berkeley-style formation by repeatedly failing to do a handstand against the appropriate part of the human pyramid. The human pyramid waited, wobbling, as I tried again and again, to do my handstand. Eventually Miss Haydock blew her whistle and (scarlet with shame) I was able to stop. Much to my surprise, Miss Haydock clearly called out, 'Well done, Pearce' (me).

Sir Terence Conran

CHAIRMAN OF STOREHOUSE

Once upon a time there was a naughty little boy called Terence Orby Conran who loved making things in wood, metal and even pottery, but he never finished anything. His mother's and father's house was strewn with half-finished pieces of furniture, drawings, paintings, and unfired pots. One day his mother got very fed up with this and said to him, 'Darling Terence Orby, you must finish that bookcase you are making. In fact, you are to stay in your room until you finish it.'

Terence Orby had a very bad temper and he started shouting at his mother, who was standing at the bottom of the stairs. She was a determined woman and insisted. He picked up the half-finished bookcase and threw it down the stairs, where it disintegrated into its component parts. (Was this the start of Knock Down furniture?)

His mother got very cross indeed and picking up the various pieces, and Terence Orby by the scruff of his neck locked him in his room, saying, 'You will stay there till you have made your bookcase.'

Terence Orby spent a considerable time sulking but, then, recognizing defeat, began to reassemble the bookcase. He worked at it with increasing enjoyment for many hours and finally, when his mother brought him a tray of supper, he had finished it. He was proud, she was proud, and they both had a sense of achievement.

The moral of this story is don't begin something unless you intend to finish it, and always do what your mother tells you to do!

John Conteh

ACTOR AND FORMER PROFESSIONAL BOXER

I remember when I was ten years old, before I had started boxing properly, my Father was teaching me to throw a double left hook; that is, a left hook to the body, followed by a left hook over the top to the chin. Well, my left to the body was alright, but the hook to the chin was never quite fast enough. He was always able to just lean back, and make me miss. Anyway, after about ten months of this, I was getting a bit frustrated. But then one day we were going through the same routine, only this time my left hook over the top to his chin was so fast, he wasn't able to get out of the way quick enough, and I hit him right on the end of the chin, with a beautiful left hook.

He was hurt a bit, but he was trying not to show it, and I remember I was a bit scared, because I felt I had done something really bad; smacking me dad on the chin felt really peculiar. But he was great about it, he just started to laugh and said, 'Well, I think you're ready to go down to the gym now.'

Above: Trevor Eve aged nine
Right: Lord Forte as a boy with his nanny
Below: Nigel Hawthorne in his perambulator

Below: Rachael Heyhoe Flint as a bridesmaid

Right: Jimmy Hill, a keen cricketer from an early age

Below right: Sir Peter Holmes aged five with Eileen 'M', a childhood friend in Budapest, Hungary

Later on that week he took me down to the Kirkby ABC, where I began my boxing career proper. It's funny but after that we never had any more boxing lessons at home.

Sue Cook

TELEVISION PRESENTER

One of my most vivid childhood memories is of a birthday party to which I was invited when I was about eight years old. I was a shy child, not one to enjoy the formality of a party surrounded by other little boys and girls I hardly knew, all of us stiffly dressed in our party best.

But I have always had a rather silly sense of humour, and when I found a pink wooden child's toilet seat upstairs in a bedroom (it was one of those which fitted over the adult lavatory seat, so that a toddler could sit on it), I thought it would be hugely entertaining to put it over my head and parade myself downstairs wearing it as a necklace.

Everyone duly laughed and commented and the joke was over. ('Time for Postman's Knock now, children.') But I could not get that toilet seat off over my head. It had seemed easy enough to get it on, but now the grown-ups gathered round me tugging and pulling, and succeeded only in bruising my chin and my nose. I just wanted the ground to open and swallow me up for good. I wanted to be anywhere in the world but there, at the party with all those children gaping at me with a mixture of hysterical amusement and horror. My spirits hit the very bottom – if you pardon the unintentional pun – when the grown-ups said there was nothing else for it but to call the Fire Brigade. I listened in appalled disbelief as somebody dialled 999. Years seemed to go by as we all sat and waited for the sound of the fire engine's bell outside.

The rest of the memory is hazy. I think my conscious mind just floated off to somewhere less painful and left the rest of me to cope as the firemen came to the room. Surely the whole world must have seen and heard them arrive. I would never live this down as long as I lived. The men in the uniforms and yellow helmets tried not to laugh, as they sliced into that hated little pink seat. I never did like parties. I still don't. And now I usually resist the temptation to liven things up by doing something silly.

Catherine Cookson
AUTHOR

But it was this ignorant man who first told me I was a writer. He didn't exactly say I was a writer, not in so many words, what he actually said was, 'It's a stinking liar you are, Katie McMullen, a stinking liar.'

I remember the day he said that to me. I was very small, and I can see myself running up the backyard and into the kitchen and going straight for him where he sat in his chair, crying, 'Granda! you know that little man you tell me about, the one that sits on the wall in Ireland no bigger than your hand, you know him? With the green jacket and the red trousers and the buckles on his shoes, and the high hat and a shillelagh as big as himself, you remember, Granda?'

'Aye, what about him?'

'Well, I've seen him, Granda.'

'Ya have?'

'Aye, Granda. He was round the top corner.'

'He was, was he? And I suppose he spoke to you?'

'Aye, Granda, he did.'

'And what did he say?'

'Well, he said "Hello, Katie." '

'He said "Hello, Katie", did he? And what did you say?'

'. . . I said "Hello, Mister, me granda knows you." '

He wiped his tash with his hand while raising his white eyebrows, then he said, 'You know what you are, Katie McMullen, don't you? You're a stinking liar. But go on, go on, don't stop, for begod! it will get you some place . . . Either into clink or into the money.'

Henry Cooper OBE
FORMER HEAVYWEIGHT BOXING CHAMPION

When my twin brother George and I lived in Bellingham, there was a fireman, Mr Hill who also lived on the estate. One day Mr Hill saw George and I sparring on the Common and suggested we joined a boxing club. He took us to Old Bellingham Amateur Boxing Club and we can therefore thank Mr Hill as he was the first one to see our potential and start us off in the boxing world.

Jilly Cooper

AUTHOR AND JOURNALIST

Here is a story about my cousin Willum, who had colossal charisma even at the age of seven when before going to prep school he rushed round gathering up all the farm workers' cigarette butts in a tin so he could have a few puffs when he reached his new school. When he got to this new school he found to his horror that all letters the boys received from home were read out by the form mistress in front of the rest of the class. One day he received a letter from our mutual grandmother:

'I saw Mummy today,' read out the form mistress in a ringing voice, and then turning over two pages by mistake she went on, 'she has a long black tail and lovely green eyes and meeows a lot.'

Willum never recovered.

Terence Cuneo

ARTIST

With artistic leanings on both sides of the family, it is hardly surprising that I inherited something of my parent's abilities. Certainly, the urge to draw was there at an early age. The first demonstration of talent took place when I was barely four.

At the time, my father, apart from magazine illustration, was also covering a number of topical subjects for the *Illustrated London News*. One day, when he had gone downstairs to lunch, I entered his studio. At once I was assailed with the entrancing smells of a studio. A pot-pourri of turpentine, canvas primer, tobacco and oil paint – delicious! On an easel was a half-tone oil drawing, just completed – still wet. The subject immediately intrigued me and I sat down to study it; a crowd of people was seen running down a street; each figure looked terrified, clearly fleeing from some fearful calamity. There were flames, smoke, broken shutters, flying stones and rubble strewn over the ground. In the foreground a fat man with a great black moustache was pushing a cart containing household possessions.

35

His moustache *fascinated* me: why, I wondered, had Poppa given only one of them a moustache like that? I pondered the question, fiercely concentrating, and was finally convinced that something should be done to rectify this omission. I picked up a brush and slapped a juicy walrus moustache on every man in the picture. So heartened was I by the splendid effect of my embellishments, that I went on to extend the improvements to the women, a baby in a pram and finally to a cat and a couple of stray dogs.

My father's reaction to these 'improvements' not only disappointed me, but also left me howling at the top of my voice nursing an extremely sore behind.

Note
To the layman, perhaps it is worth explaining that to paint on top of a *still wet canvas* meant that my father was forced to repaint every single face in the picture! Now, as a mature painter myself, I can *well* understand what this meant to him in extra work and frustration. I think I would have killed the little brute!!

Peter Cushing
ACTOR

I burst into this world on a Monday morning, weighing in at a record 10½ lbs. in Kenley, Surrey – then no more than a village but now, I imagine, all but swallowed up by the sprawling suburbia of the 'Great Wen'. I was apparently ravenous from the word go, arriving in time for an early breakfast, and much of my childhood was spent foraging for food, to keep me going between proper meals. My mother always maintained that I had hollow legs.

One of those supplementary snacks was raw bacon-rind, which I would suck in the garden. Once, to Mother's horror, I came in happily sucking a long, juicy worm, having dropped the original delicacy and picked up the unfortunate invertebrate by mistake. I suppose I was about two at the time, my palate and perception not sufficiently developed to notice any difference.

When I was old enough, I would volunteer to go shopping for Mother, always with a wistful 'Can I keep the change?' – invariably granted, depending upon the amount involved.

'. . . and a penn'orth of broken biscuits, please,' I would add, after I'd given the grocer the official order. In those days, long before the era of pre-packaging, this was a most profitable purchase, being presented with a large paper bag full of every imaginable biscuit, which had not withstood the journey from bakery to retailer. These would be consumed on the walk back, but having a sweet tooth, I wasn't too keen on the cheese varieties, so they were scattered to the birds. Sometimes there was a preponderance of these, as they were less resilient to transportation than my favourites, but I lacked the courage to return and lodge a complaint with the shop-keeper. And anyway, the birds were grateful, and made good company with their perky twitterings.

If there happened to be a freshly baked loaf on the list of family requirements, it didn't remain intact for very long, the aroma proving too much for my susceptibilities, and great hunks of the staff of life would be missing by the time I got home. I was always delighted if it happened to be a 'cottage loaf' because the whole of the smaller 'bun' could be removed and devoured, leaving the larger portion looking less as if mice had been at it.

I had a curious habit in my gastronomic feats at the dining-table. Having a fully equipped doll's house – presumably a hang-over from the days before I was 'defrocked' – I would eat my meals using the miniature cutlery, measuring approximately 1½ inches. My parents never objected to this eccentricity, unless there was company present, because – although it took me a considerable time to wade through my huge helpings (I was still on 'firsts' when they were tucking into 'seconds') – it meant I didn't 'gobble my food', which was rightly considered good for the digestion.

One Christmas, as a special treat, I was taken to a London theatre to see *Peter Pan*, and fell quite desperately in love with Peter. Since *He* was always played by a She, that really wasn't as bad as it sounds, although I'm sure Freud (perhaps even Aunt Maude) would have found something to say on the subject.

For many weeks after this enchanted evening, I would fling the window wide open when I went up to bed and kneel before it, cocooned in a counterpane, praying for him to come flying through, teach me how to fly and take me back to see the 'Never, Never, Never Land'. Mother often found me asleep in this attitude of prayer, the bedroom as cold as the outside of an igloo, and, like Puccini's Mimi, my tiny hands frozen.

Roald Dahl

AUTHOR

In 1920, when I was still only three, my mother's eldest child, my own sister Astri, died from appendicitis. She was seven years old when she died, which was also the age of my own eldest daughter, Olivia, when she died from measles forty-two years later.

Astri was far and away my father's favourite. He adored her beyond measure and her sudden death left him literally speechless for days afterwards. He was so overwhelmed with grief that when he himself went down with pneumonia a month or so afterwards, he did not care whether he lived or died.

If they had had penicillin in those days, neither appendicitis nor pneumonia would have been so much of a threat, but with no penicillin or any other magical antibiotic cures, pneumonia in particular was a very dangerous illness indeed. The pneumonia patient, on about the fourth or fifth day, would invariably reach what was known as 'the crisis'. The temperature soared and the pulse became rapid. The patient had to fight to survive. My father refused to fight. He was thinking, I am quite sure, of his beloved daughter, and he was wanting to join her in heaven. So he died. He was fifty-seven years old.

My mother had now lost a daughter and a husband all in the space of a few weeks. Heaven knows what it must have felt like to be hit with a double catastrophe like this. Here she was, a young Norwegian in a foreign land, suddenly having to face all alone the very gravest problems and responsibilities. She had five children to look after, three of her own and two by her husband's first wife, and to make matters worse, she herself was expecting another baby in two months' time. A less courageous woman would almost certainly have sold the house and packed her bags and headed straight back to Norway with the children. Over there in her own country she had her mother and father willing and waiting to help her, as well as her two unmarried sisters. But she refused to take the easy way out. Her husband had always stated most emphatically that he wished all his children to be educated in English schools. They were the best in the world, he used to say. Better by far than the Norwegian ones. Better even than the Welsh ones, despite the fact that he lived in Wales and had his business there. He maintained that

38

there was some kind of magic about English schooling and that the education it provided had caused the inhabitants of a small island to become a great nation and a great Empire and to produce the world's greatest literature. 'No child of mine', he kept saying, 'is going to school anywhere else but in England.' My mother was determined to carry out the wishes of her dead husband.

To accomplish this, she would have to move house from Wales to England. but she wasn't ready for that yet. She must stay here in Wales for a while longer, where she knew people who could help and advise her, especially her husband's great friend and partner, Mr Aadnesen. But even if she wasn't leaving Wales quite yet, it was essential that she move to a smaller and more manageable house. She had enough children to look after without having to bother about a farm as well. So as soon as her fifth child (another daughter) was born, she sold the big house and moved to a smaller one a few miles away in Llandaff. It was called Cumberland Lodge and it was nothing more than a pleasant medium-sized surburban villa. So it was in Llandaff two years later, when I was six years old, that I went to my first school.

The school was a kindergarten run by two sisters. Mrs Corfield and Miss Tucker, and it was called Elmtree House. It is astonishing how little one remembers about one's life before the age of seven or eight. I can tell you all sorts of things that happened to me from eight onwards, but only very few before that. I went for a whole year to Elmtree House but I cannot even remember what my classroom looked like. Nor can I picture the faces of Mrs Corfield or Miss Tucker, although I am sure they were sweet and smiling. I do have a blurred memory of sitting on the stairs and trying over and over again to tie one of my shoelaces, but that is all that comes back to me at this distance of the school itself.

On the other hand, I can remember very clearly the journeys I made to and from the school because they were so tremendously exciting. Great excitement is probably the only thing that really interests a six-year-old-boy and it sticks in his mind. In my case, the excitement centred around my new tricycle. I rode to school on it every day with my eldest sister riding on hers. No grown-ups came with us, and I can remember oh so vividly how the two of us used to go racing at enormous tricycle speeds down the middle of the road and then, most glorious of all, when we came to a corner, we would lean to one side and take it on two wheels. All this, you must realize, was in the good old days when the sight of a motor-car on the street was an event, and it was quite safe for tiny children to go tricycling and whooping their way to school in the centre of the highway.

So much, then, for my memories of kindergarten sixty-two years ago. It's not much, but it's all there is left.

Tessa Dahl
AUTHOR AND JOURNALIST

What a wonderful childhood. What a wonderful father. What a wonderful mother. Buckinghamshire, an orchard full of cows and an aviary abundant with homing budgerigars. My father would let them out at seven o'clock in the morning. A flock of yellow, green, blue and white birds with swallow-like wings would dart around the garden, settling in the willow trees as my father herded us into the car (an old grey Humber) and off to school.

Driving along every morning, Daddy would make us sing out our times tables. Once we had proved we knew them the reward came – a story. Oh lucky children, that's what we were. Filled with spark and bubbling like little pots of melted chocolate never left to cool.

Secrets of the household at last revealed. My glorious mother would wander around in her dressing gown until midday, drinking cups of coffee (ah, is that where I learnt the art?), while my father was up and dressed by six thirty, working in his hut in the orchard by nine o'clock. That hut, with its polystyrene walls, fraying lino floor and battered furniture. The oasis of a genius. We were forbidden ever to disturb him when he was working, the cows would stick their heads through his windows unaware of this rule and eat his curtains. There was a cairn of cigarette butts outside the door.

Chocolate, a ritual. There had to be a full 'Choccie Box' at all times. My father's favourites, Kit Kat, Aero and the Flake. After each meal my mother would ceremoniously carry the 'Choccie Box' to my father, who, with the precision of a *maître chef* chopping his *legumes*, would operate on each bar. A tiny slice of each.

At five o'clock the budgerigars would be put to bed, a lobster pot dropped into their hatch. In single file each bird would take its turn, line up and drop down into the aviary. Heads under wings.

Our heads went under our wings with satisfied exhaustion. My mother would sing 'So I say Goodnight Sweetheart' in her husky voice and dance out of the room. This was followed by my father. He would pace our bedroom and with each step a glorious sentence filled with fantasy and brilliance would spill out. Before we slept we heard 'James and the Giant Peach' and 'Charlie and the Chocolate Factory' – and we were the first.

Joanna David
ACTRESS

When I was four years old, my dancing school in Altrincham, Cheshire, gave their annual dancing display at the Garrick Theatre. I was to play a pearl in a sea ballet and my mother embroidered hundreds of pearls onto a pink net costume to make me as 'pearl-like' as possible.

The night arrived and I started the ballet underneath a high oyster shell, hidden from view, with a grown-up mermaid who was there to remind me when to emerge.

Unfortunately my fright and excitement demanded that I went to 'the loo' way before my big moment, so I was led across the stage by an embarrassed mermaid and duly led back again and placed back under the shell, much to my shame! Never to be forgotten!

Michael Denison
ACTOR

At the end of the First World War when I was about three, the uncle who brought me up was so seriously ill that we had two nurses living in the house. My poor aunt – my dead mother's eldest sister – was both worried and exhausted and one of the nurses took me out for the afternoon to give her the chance of a rest. 'We'll get some flowers for her, shall we?' the nurse said to me. And on our return I was launched, well scrubbed, into my aunt's presence at tea-time clutching a small bunch of carnations – watched encouragingly by the actual donor. 'See what I've buyed for myself!' I said proudly, and refused to be parted from the gift!

Dame Daphne du Maurier
AUTHOR

We passed under the archway and came to the house at the end of the small court, on the right-hand side. There were steps leading up to the white front-door, and the bell had to be rung so that the nurse could be helped to lift the pram up the steps and into the hall. The nurse was dressed in grey, and she wore a black bonnet on her head with a veil stretched tightly across her face. Ellison, the parlour maid, wore a cream-coloured uniform, and she had a frilly cap and apron. They chatted a moment, exclaiming over the weight of the pram, while the baby within peered up at them, rosy-cheeked, smiling. Angela and I marched inside. Then I saw, to my dismay, coats and hats in the hall, and from the drawing-room to the left of the long narrow entrance came the sound of laughter and talking. This meant there were people to lunch. We should be summoned later to say how-do-you-do and to shake hands. Angela turned inquiringly to the parlour-maid, not minding, but I hurried upstairs to be out of the way, while Nurse lifted Baby from the pram.

The stairs conquered, I paused on the first-floor landing and looked over my shoulder down to the hall. Doors were opening. The talking was louder. I turned quickly to the right, and putting my hand on the banister pulled my way up our own short twisting flight of stairs to the nursery floor. There was a gate, standing open. Beyond was safety. I ran at once into the day-nursery, the familiar warmth and smell of it bringing intense relief: here were the doll's house, the toy-cupboard with two shelves – one for Angela, one for me – the cretonne-covered toy-box, an old armchair that could be turned at will into a large ship wrecked at sea, and so into the wider part of the room, with the table set for lunch, the fire burning behind the high brass guard, and the wide window overlooking Albany Street and the barracks.

'Now then, no dawdling, hat and coat off, and hands washed before lunch.'

The nurse had reached the top of our stairs with Baby. But I wanted to look down into Albany Street. The Life Guards might be coming back from their outing, breast-plates gleaming, plumes proudly waving from their helmets. It was the bugle-call that used to awaken us every morning, in the little room we shared, Angela and I, once I was promoted from the night-nursery across the passage after Baby was born.

> 'Tra-la-la, tra-la-la, tra-la-la-la.
> Tra-la-la, tra-la-la, tra-la-la-la.
> Tra-la-la, tra-la-la, tra-la-la-LAAAAA!'

Nurse said it was called *Reveille*, but I knew what the bugle was saying. It said:

> 'Bring in your horses and give them to drink,
> Bring in your horses and give them to drink,
> Bring in your horses and give them to DRINK . . .'

Such groomings there must be, such polishing of brass, such clattering of hoofs, such quenching of thirst from the great troughs inside the barracks. It made something to think about before getting-up time, and having to dress in the cold bedroom, and going through to the night-nursery to be washed and have teeth cleaned, and worst of all the beastly rags pulled out of my hair which were put there to make it curl, though they never did.

Breakfast would follow. 'Now don't mess about with your spoon. Eat up your porridge.' I did not like porridge. It made me feel sick. Lumpy, slimy, horrid. 'If you were a little poor child always hungry you would be glad to eat your porridge.' But I wasn't a little poor child, and saying that didn't make me eat it up. I wished the poor child could have it, not me.

'I don't care.'

This was rude, and I might be punished for it. Made to stand in the corner, perhaps, and so not have to eat the porridge. But the nurse, whose name was Nurse Rush and who had replaced the much-loved nanny – we were not told why – contented herself with a snub.

> 'Don't Care was made to care,
> Don't Care was hung,
> Don't Care was put in a pot
> And cooked till he was done.'

I thought for a moment, then poked once more at the porridge. Who was Don't Care, I wondered? Not a poor child. No, he sounded more like a little old man, rather tubby, who lived alone in a hut, and then some cruel people came and put him in this great black pot and hung it over a fire, which made a sizzling noise. Poor Don't Care ... Did he scream? Or did some nice person come and rescue him? What happened next? But they never told you. Grown-ups started something interesting and would not finish. If you asked they said, 'That will do now,' which was the end of it.

Don't Care was made to care. I was on his side. And he became real, like the boy in *Reading Steps*, which I was trying to master. 'Dan Ran To The Man.' But why did Dan run to the man? Was somebody after him? Was he being chased by a wolf? Meg Had A Sore Leg. Silly thing, perhaps she had fallen down, and then made a fuss. I saw her sitting on her bed and crying. Ben Had A Fat Hen. He must have found it hard to hold, and then I expect it squawked, and flew out of his arms, and went fluttering off into a farmyard. If only I could read the longer words in the end pages they might tell me more about Dan and Meg and Ben, but the letters in these words were all joined together, not like the big letters.

I liked H. It was a gate, over which I could climb. And A was a swing I could sit on. B was a fat loaf. and G was a half-round like C, but had a little seat. One day soon the big letters would join on to the small letters and I should understand each one, and be able to read the writing in books and not just look at pictures. And then, and then ...

'Do you want to go somewhere?'

'No.'

'Then what are you wriggling for?'

'I don't know . . .' I was thinking of Dan Ran To The Man and what might have happened, and it made me excited, but they don't understand, and she drags me to the night-nursery and pulls down my knickers and makes me sit on the chamberpot, and this is the most shaming thing of all – not even down to the bathroom, but stuck there, on the pot, like Baby. And the pot is too small. I spill what I do.

Then suddenly, it's not after breakfast but after lunch (which also made me feel sick, those horrid greens and the rice pudding), and, 'Hurry up, now, you're to go downstairs and say how-do-you-do'.

Hands and face scrubbed, hair brushed, and down we go to the dreaded dining-room. Angela is beaming, why doesn't she mind? Baby is smiling too, she is being carried, so she is safe. The dining-room door is opened. The ladies are all at lunch. Lots of them. They all wear hats, which makes it worse. Even Mummy has a hat, giving her an unfamiliar look. Nurse Rush puts Baby in her arms, and Baby coos. The ladies all turn and look.

'Oh, aren't they *sweet*?'

But we're not sweet. At least, I'm not. Angela may be, prancing up to each lady in turn and shaking hands, and Baby, being given sugar from the coffee-tray, but I am Don't Care, and Dan, and I hate them all, and when they suddenly get up from the table to go into the drawing-room they are much too tall, they speak too loudly, they laugh too much, and it's always the same, Grown-Ups are too big, too noisy and, worse besides, they want to kiss me. I turn my face away.

'Oh, she's shy.'

I'm not shy. I hate you, that's all. And I don't want to be kissed. I start tearing at my nails.

'Ah-ha! I can see a little girl who bites her nails.'

'Yes, she will do it. We've tried bitter aloes, but it doesn't stop her.'

Mummy shakes her head reproachfully. She pops another piece of coffee sugar into Baby's mouth. P'raps if they gave me sugar and not bitter aloes . . . Then they are all in the drawing-room, still talking, still laughing, and when nobody is looking I run out of the room and upstairs, away to the safe nursery, and here at least they won't follow. Even Nurse Rush must be down below with Ellison and Alice the cook in the basement kitchen, also talking, also laughing.

45

Peter Duncan
ACTOR

My most vivid memory is singing the songsheet on stage in my father's pantomime at the age of two – 'How many legs has daddy long legs got . . .'

The memory flashed back as my own two-year-old clambered on stage at the Hackney Empire this year to say it with her daddy: 'I've got two, a cow's got four, a worm's got none, and a shrimp's got more . . .'

In fact, I used the very same words on a big rolled-up sheet which was lost in the loft:

You may know how many beans make five
Think you know a lot . . . OH!'

It was as though thirty-five years passed in a moment.

The Rt. Hon. The Earl of Dunraven and Mount-Earl
FARMER AND BLOODSTOCK BREEDER

Many childhood memories flash through one's mind, none of which make up many lines, so here are a few that have stayed in my memory.

Working miracles
or realizing that God does not always work miracles
When going to school on the Cork to Fishguard boat, I would say my prayers as the boat left the River Lee, begging God that when I awoke in the morning at 3.00a.m. the boat would be sailing towards Cork and not moored alongside cold, wet Fishguard. My plea for a miracle always went unheard and God went down the league of popularity.

Gone up in smoke
Having been brought up surrounded by horses and haybarns and always on the lookout, as a youngster, for somewhere to smoke the odd cigarette, my father's severe warning always

46

comes to mind. It was that if he caught me smoking in the hay barn, it wasn't me he was worried about, getting burned to death, but the loss of the hay for feeding the animals. That warning sank in, so I never smoked in the hay barns, but usually in the chicken house – poor chickens.

Rosalind Erskine

AUTHORESS

Lament for a Ruined Childhood

They took me to school in September;
   The three of us went in the Rolls.
It's a day I shall always remember
   'Cos I knew that *my combies had holes.*

I went with the rest to the dorm;
   We knelt and we prayed for our souls.
But I was the butt of the form
   'Cos they saw that *my combies had holes.*

At hockey I played for the school,
   Scoring goals upon goals upon goals;
But afterwards I was the fool
   'Cos they knew that *my combies had holes.*

The fields which we played on were dotted
   By hills that were made by the moles;
The moles had a laugh, 'cos they spotted
   That all of *my combies had holes.*

There were ponies, and plentiful riding,
   There were mares, and occasional foals;
But even the foals were deriding –
   They guessed that *my combies had holes.*

At Drama I acted with vision,
   Playing roles upon roles upon roles,
But the audience laughed in derision
   'Cos they heard that *my combies had holes.*

We learned about sewing and cooking,
    And arrangements of flowers in bowls,
But the eyes of the needles were looking
    To see if *my combies had holes*.

Oh mothers of daughters, have pity!
    Oh drag them no more through the coals!
'Cos nobody's daughter is pretty
    When she knows that *her combies have holes*.

Kenny Everett

RADIO AND TELEVISION PERSONALITY

I always remember my childhood days as being constantly sunny. It always seemed to be sunny. Even in winter, when the rest of the kids and I were clustered in the classroom praying for snow, it always seemed sunny. There were no yellow lines either in those days, so you could park anywhere. Except of course, we didn't have anything to park!

Our idea of a good time in those dim, distant days, was swinging on the lamp post outside our house. Ah, the thrill of running home from school with your coat tied around your neck, imitating the Cisco Kid, just in order to swing on a lamp post! Nowadays, of course, it's all computer games. And watches that turn into robots that turn into cars that turn into side-streets!

I also remember running a lot. When I was a child at school, I was constantly amazed at the fact that grown-ups never ran anywhere, they always walked. Kids of course being terribly impatient, *never* walked but ran. Always pelting, full-tilt around corners.

Nowadays, I go ten times as fast without moving anything but my accelerator foot! I love my BMW. Not only does it save on shoe-leather, but it's got a hi-fi inside and a heater and it's terribly comfortable. There are definite compensations for getting old!

Major Ronald Ferguson

On many occasions during the holidays I was taken to visit my grandparents Brigadier and Mrs Algernon Ferguson who lived at Polebrook Hall near Oundle, Northamptonshire. Polebrook Hall was large with long dark gloomy corridors which was perfect for my elder brother John and I to play all sorts of extravagant games usually based on speed with the inevitable accident and tears. At that time my grandfather was only able to get around his beautiful and large garden by means of an electric wheelchair.

The garden had many gravelled paths with beautiful lawns sloping down to a large lake with every known species of duck enjoying the peace and quiet of such a beautiful and natural haven. It was always a particular delight to be taken on rides by my grandfather. I would sit down at his feet but on special occasions I would sit on his lap and steer the chair and inevitably try to go faster than grandfather required. To go faster you turned a handle to the right over four marks at which point your handle met a large retaining pin which stopped any more movement or speed.

Every afternoon grandfather had a rest for about two hours and needless to say this was the moment to sneak out for my private excursions around the gardens in the chair. I think on reflection that everyone including grandfather knew about my excursions but as it was not hurting or even worrying anyone the blind eyes were turned.

Inevitably I craved for more speed and one afternoon having set a time trial course which wound up and down the lawns all around the lake and around the herbaceous borders I was determined to beat my record. All went well until I managed to get the speed handle over the retaining screw thinking erroneously that this meant more speed. Alas, no more speed but disaster. I couldn't get the handle back over the screw. Youthful panic set in. Whilst struggling with the handle my course was erratic, to put it mildly, dozing ducks were scattered and gardeners were running to create even greater chaos. The inevitable happened, my steering eventually failed and straight into the lake I went.

Grandfather was informed which resulted in being sent to my room after a dose of a leather belt. Sadly, the chair never worked again and was eventually changed for a petrol engined one with an ignition key. Regretfully I never found the key hiding place however much I tried. A great time with a wonderful grandfather. The memories are still very vivid and I can still feel the leather belt and never broke my course record.

Admiral of the Fleet
Sir John Fieldhouse GCB,GBE
FORMER FIRST SEA LORD AND CHIEF OF THE DEFENCE STAFF

I learned the art of getting other people to work for me at an early age, in kindergarten in fact, when sat down and told to knit a dishcloth using large wooden needles and a ball of string. I quickly discovered that I made best progress by dropping a stitch and taking it up to the mistress. She would then do three more rows, whilst correcting my error, which was more than I could do in a week! The same technique has been working for me ever since!

Sir Ranulph Fiennes, Bt.
EXPLORER

A Childhood Poem

When I was six in Constantia, South Africa I was a member of a little gang of six local children (all Afrikaanse) and we composed a gang song which we sang as we traipassed about in the woods and vines clasping bamboos. Somehow the lyrics have survived three decades despite my sieve-like memory. The gang was known as the Mealie (Corn Cob) Band.

> Mealie Pop, Mealie Pop, Mealie. Round the Rio Grande.
> Mealie Pop, Mealie Pop, Mealie. Singing to the Mealie
> Band.
> Up the Rocky Mountains to the slushy swamps of Mideon.
> The Mealie Band. The Mealie Band. Like the mighty hosts
> of Gideon.

Mealie Pop, Mealie Pop, Mealie. Muscles large and
    strong,
Rippling with valour and singing loud and long.
Through the misty Punjab to the dusty streets of Wongs.
They trek the Kalahari and soon they reach the Congo.

Mealie Pop, Mealie Pop, Mealie. Round the Rio Grande.
Mealie Pop, Mealie Pop, Mealie. Singing to the Mealie
    Band.
Up the Rocky Mountains to the slushy swamps of Mideon.
The Mealie Band. The Mealie Band. Like the mighty hosts
    of Gideon.

Nothing else distinct of those carefree days remains.

Lord Forte

CHAIRMAN OF TRUSTEHOUSE FORTE PLC

One of the childhood memories that comes to me is at the age of
ten in Scotland when I made my first proposal of marriage. It
was to the prettiest girl in my class, who was called Mary
Stephenson. Her reply, when it came, was blunt.

'My mother says I cannot marry you because you are an
Italian.'

I replied, 'Can't marry an Italian? I've got a castle in Italy. You
tell your mother that.'

[P.S. I did not, of course, have a castle in Italy.]

The Rt. Hon. Norman Fowler MP

SECRETARY OF STATE FOR EMPLOYMENT

I don't know whether they were my formative years but
certainly I spent my earliest years under a Morrison shelter. For
those who don't know (and they must be very many now) a
Morrison shelter was a great steel table which was an internal air
raid shelter. Issued during the Second World War the idea was
that although a bomb might collapse your house as long as you

were in your shelter you could escape injury. Our shelter dominated the backroom. It served as a table but just as surely it served as a sleeping place and in Chelmsford where I was brought up this was no bad precaution.

Chelmsford had two disadvantages during the war. The first was that it housed both Marconis and the Hoffmanns who made ball bearings. It was a favourite target and certainly in the first part of the war, raids were reasonably commonplace. One of my earliest memories is of the back gardens in our street being splattered with fire from a low-flying aircraft. The second disadvantage was that Chelmsford was on the way to London. Not only did aircraft drop their load too early but also the later German rockets did not always make their destination.

Through all these troubles the Morrison shelter in the back room stood up marvellously. Ceilings came down upon it but it was always secure. On one night there was such an almighty bang that my mother thought the whole house was about to come down. In fact the bomb had dropped a street away. It reduced the house to rubble. Mercifully the family were in their Morrison shelter and once the rescue workers had cleared it away they emerged totally unscathed. The Morrison shelter may not have been a thing of beauty – but it worked.

The Rt. Hon. the Lord Gibson-Watt
MC, JP, DL

My first memory was walking to fetch the papers from the station aged about four and on the way picking up the spent cartridges from what is now the A470. In those days it was not properly macadamized. A horse towed the tar sprayer and I can still smell the tar.

My father who died when I was eleven or twelve used to take me for a walk on Sunday afternoons. Once I found a dead hedgehog – the stench was bad. 'Spit', advised my father. 'Always do if you get a really bad smell.'

With a brother and two cousins we built a wigwam out of Douglas fir branches and then I lit a fire inside it. I was surprised that the wigwam went up in flames and we only just got out.

Gary Glitter
POP SINGER

It was the day before the family Christmas party, which would consist of aunts, uncles and cousins dressed in fancy costume. Among all the food in the parlour being prepared for the grand occasion, I had seen for the first time a jelly. A large wobbly jelly and I was anxious to touch and taste it.

To delay the excitement, my Auntie Pat decided to take me in my pushchair on a trip around the town where I lived. Eventually, we came to a halt outside the ladies' toilets below Banbury Town Hall. She put the brake on and left me at the top of the stone stairs.

I was two and a half years old and being an inquisitive child I managed to escape, in true Houdini style, from the harness for which these contraptions are infamous and ventured into the bowels of the building. My entrance to this 'Secret Ladies' Place' suddenly became overshadowed by a terrible sense of shock. I had tumbled down the flight of stairs, fallen flat on my face and had lost my tongue. I was speechless.

My aunt quickly ran, with me in one hand and my tongue in the other, to the nearest St John's Ambulance station, which was strategically placed next to the town hall. They wizzed me off to the local hospital – everything seemed to be moving so fast. Lots of huge faces were peering at me, talking about me, when suddenly an object, much like a colander, was placed over my face. As I drifted under all I could think of was the large jelly, waiting patiently for me.

It seemed that the apparatus used to cover my face was for the 'gas'. It seemed to have a rhythm all of its own.

> Wish e lah, lah, lah, I could have some jelly,
> Wish e lah, lah, lah, I could have some jelly,

When I awoke I was stitched up. Well and truly stitched up. My tongue was swollen and hanging down to my chin. My vocabulary had shrunk to the occasional 'ugh' (which later in my life served me well when writing my first song). I left the hospital and arrived home in time to hear the joyous singing. Everyone seemed to be laughing, talking and eating except for me. I was desperately trying to eat the prized jelly through a straw, while sticking my tongue out at whoever looked at me.

Martyn Goff
AUTHOR, CRITIC, BOOKSELLER AND BROADCASTER

When I was nine years of age my parents divorced. My mother was shattered by this emotionally, apart from losing her beautiful house, staff and the like. She fled to Australia for six months, taking me, her youngest by eight years, with her.

We travelled on the *Oronsay*, an Orient Line vessel where, so I am told, I was pretty insufferable. One day I accosted a rather chubby, pipe-smoking Englishman on deck and demanded that he play deck quoits with me. He refused. I repeated my demand loudly enough to attract the attention of other passengers, so he gave in. I beat him and loudly proclaimed my triumph.

As I walked away from him, two elderly ladies stopped me and asked whether I knew whom I had been playing with. I shook my head. 'J.B. Priestley,' they said in awe. Of course, it meant nothing to me.

Years later I got to know Priestley a little and finally told him the story. To my surprise he remembered the incident vividly. 'You were quite the most bumptious and tiresome little boy I had ever met,' he said, 'and I was furious at losing to you!'

David Gower
LEICESTERSHIRE AND ENGLAND CRICKETER

I was brought up in what was then Tanganyika, now Tanzania, for the first five years of my life. One early problem was coming back out of the sea at Dar-es-Salaam to be confronted with two apparently similar-looking women, one of whom was my mother. Faced with the same odds as tossing a coin at the start of a cricket match, I called wrong, probably as much to the embarrassment of my mother as I.

What however did stand out as a childhood memory was our tour of the North Tanganyika game parks; the Ngorongoro Crater and Lake Manyara, where, despite being charged by elephants, watching buffalo stampede and trying to ease myself out of the opposite side of the Land-Rover to a rhino, my current interest in the conservation of the world's wildlife was born.

Dulcie Gray CBE

ACTRESS AND WRITER

I was at boarding school in Wallingford at the age of three and a half, and by four years old had been given an illustrated Bible. I especially loved the picture of white-bearded, white-robed God. 'He is everywhere,' I was told, but try as hard as I could, I couldn't find him.

'He is always in church,' I was assured, 'because that is His House.'

Once again I drew blank. Then one day when the vicar of Wallingford was away on holiday, we were taken to nearby Mongewell Church. We were put into old-fashioned pews with high surrounds, from which, even sitting on a hassock, I could see nothing of the service while it was on ground level. The Reverend Hughes slowly and majestically climbed the pulpit steps to deliver his sermon. He was in white robes, and had a white beard.

'Hurray! There's God!' I shouted happily. I was not popular.

Lucinda Green MBE

My very first memory – I was playing in the attic playroom of the house my mother was brought up in Scotland. A yellow flash streaked across the sky. I remember leaping up and rushing to the window shouting 'What's that *lellow* thing?' I was four at the time and that is my earliest memory.

My next most important memory was about a year later, again staying away from home and reading a picture book to myself in bed. Suddenly I realized that the word 'YELLOW' made sense to my eyes and thence to my tongue. From that moment on I found I could read properly.

By sheer coincidence, the colours in which I have ridden cross country for as long as I have competed have been yellow.

Graham Greene OM, CH
AUTHOR

Of all my first six years I have only such random memories as
these and I cannot be sure of the time-sequence. They are
significant for me because they remain, the stray symbols of a
dream after the story has sunk back into the unconscious, and
they cry for rescue like the survivors of a shipwreck.

There was a particular kind of wheaten biscuit with a very pale
pure unsweetened flavour – I am reminded now of the Host –
which only my mother had the right to eat. They were kept in a
special biscuit tin in her bedroom and sometimes as a favour I
was given one to eat dipped in milk. I associate my mother with
a remoteness, which I did not at all resent, and with a smell of
eau-de-cologne. If I could have tasted her I am sure she would
have tasted of wheaten biscuits. She paid occasional state visits
to the nursery in the School House, a large confused room which
looked out on the flint church and the old cemetery, with toy
cupboards and bookshelves and a big wooden rocking-horse
with wicked eyes and one large comfortable wicker-chair for the
nurse beside the steel fireguard, and my mother gained in my
eyes great dignity from her superintendence of the linen-
cupboard, where a frightening witch lurked. The wheaten
biscuit remains for me a symbol of her cool puritan beauty – she
seemed to eliminate all confusion, to recognize the good from
the bad and choose the good, though where her family was
concerned in later years she noticed only the good. If one of us
had committed murder she would, I am sure, have blamed the
victim. When she was in an untroubled coma before death and I
was watching by her bed, her long white plantagenet face
reminded me of a crusader on a tomb. It seemed the right
peaceful end for the tall calm beautiful girl standing in a punt in
a long skirt with a tiny belted waist and wearing a straw boater
whom I had seen in the family album.

Until I had grown up I think my only real moments of
affection for my father were when he made frog-noises with his
palms, or played Fly Away, Jack, Fly Away, Jill, with a piece of
sticking-plaster on his finger, or made me blow open the lid
of his watch. Only when I had children of my own did I realize
how his interest in my doings had been genuine, and only then I

56

discovered a buried love and sorrow for him, which emerges today from time to time in dreams.

I think that my parents' was a very loving marriage; how far any marriage is happy is another matter and beyond an outsider's knowledge. Happiness can be ruined by children, by financial difficulties, by so many secret things: love too can be ruined, but I think their love withstood the pressure of six children and great anxieties.

Dame Beryl Grey DBE

FORMER PRIMA BALLERINA, THE ROYAL BALLET

I had my first big bitter disappointment when I was nine. I developed mumps on the morning of an audition for a dance scholarship at the R.A.D. (Royal Academy of Dancing) which would offer one free class a week. I cried for several hours. A month later my teacher arranged an audition instead at the Sadler's Wells Ballet School where I gained a four-year scholarship and an option to join the company following that daily training if I was suitable. I feel fate arranged it all for I was to be with Sadler's Wells Company until I was twenty-nine years old (later known as The Royal Ballet). So out of an apparent misfortune came something wonderful which of course shaped and decided my career.

Sir Eldon Griffiths MP

POLITICIAN

'The Best Breakfast I ever ate'

When I first came back to England, after many years in the United States, I kept a herd of a thousand pigs at a very small farm in Sussex. I've often wondered why; but one reason, I am sure, was Uncle Tom.

Uncle Tom was a former naval person. He ran away from school just in time to join the Fleet in the Battle of Jutland. He then served in a line of battleships whose names – *Revenge, Hood, Rodney* – stirred my imagination when, as a boy, I would go to see him on the bridge of his ship during Navy Days in

Plymouth. Later, when he came home from the sea, Uncle Tom bought a cottage in Cornwall. He kept a large sow named Gertie in the sty next door. Gertie was my first pig. I loved her enough willingly to clean her 'quarters', as Uncle Tom called the sty. Sometimes he and I would walk her down the lane on a leash which he attached to her collar.

Gertie's job was to produce piglets. How exactly this was done I was too young to be told, but looking back, I can only assume that the real purpose of Gertie's leash was to enable Uncle Tom to take her to the next-door farmyard where Ole Downing, or RY as we called the farmer, owned a boar called Ephraim.

At first I used to cry when Gertie's piglets were taken to market. But after Uncle Tom explained that the piglets didn't really mind because their willing sacrifice meant that hungry little children, all over England, could have bacon each morning for breakfast, I hardened my heart and became just as keen as he was on fattening up the piglets for market.

In those days, of course, there was rationing. And bacon for breakfast was a treat. So when, during the school holidays, I visited Uncle Tom and showed him my reports which, for once, put me at the top of my class, I was delighted to hear him say that next morning he would cook me the best plate of bacon in the world.

I couldn't wait to get out of bed the next day. And when I went downstairs Uncle Tom was waiting. He took me into the larder. Hanging from a hook in the ceiling was the biggest side of bacon you've ever seen. Fifty years later, I can still see and smell that side of bacon: it was succulent, juicy and smoked to a rich golden brown.

'A boy who is top of his class can cut off his own slice, thick as he likes', said Uncle Tom. And he took out the long sailor's knife which he used to cut plugs of black tobacco for his pipe.

'Use this', he said, 'it's sharp.'

What an honour it was! Uncle Tom lifted me up and showed me where to cut not one but three thick slices off the best part of that side of bacon. And when I'd done so, he fried it, with two eggs and three pieces of bread.

I don't think I've ever eaten so magnificent a breakfast, not even on British Rail or at Claridges. I remember polishing it off by cleaning the plate with a crust: delicious!

Then, afterwards, I went out to see Gertie. Horrors, her sty was empty! Racing back to the cottage I shouted at the top of my voice: 'Uncle Tom, Uncle Tom, Gertie's got away'.

Uncle Tom smiled a sad naval smile. He took me by the hand. 'You've just eaten a slice of Gertie', he told me. 'Didn't I promise that a good boy would have the best bacon breakfast in the world?'

Ralph Hammond Innes CBE

AUTHOR

The Cat

Things that stay in the mind . . . The first wasp sting, readings from *Black Beauty* by the old kitchen range of a house in the Causeway at Horsham where I was born, my mother literally in tears as she described the carthorse down in the Carfax and thrashing with its hooves, my nurse-maid giggling at the foreign soldiers marching to church. Portuguese. I remember distinctly they were Portuguese. And riding the vicar's daughter's bicycle down across the river bridge to lie in the grass by the boundary line and watch men in white fool around with bat and ball – Sussex playing another county.

There were dark passages to that old house and the roof was of Horsham stone, great moss-grown slabs of it. But it is the passage beyond my bedroom door I remember, the dark journey to the loo, the ghostly figures lurking – and the bathroom. I don't know why I locked the cat in the bathroom. I suppose I didn't like it. Or maybe I was bored. The fact remains that I did, and then forgot all about the poor little beast.

It was my mother who found it and my father who beat me – on the bare bum with the back of a long-handled hairbrush. It was the only time he ever raised a hand to me and it was that more than the hurt that made an indelible impression, for he was a mild-mannered, kindly man. I have never locked a cat in a bathroom since!

Jan Harvey
ACTRESS

Imagine my mother's pride when, at the age of six, I was chosen to sing the solo song at the Sunday School concert.

By the NINTH verse, however, even her adoration had severely palled. Perhaps this is why, even today, when asked to speak or do anything publicly, I err on the side of brevity!

The Rt. Hon. Roy Hattersley MP
DEPUTY LEADER OF THE LABOUR PARTY

Some time during the late 1930s I acquired my first lead soldiers – not 'sets' in Britain's boxes of eight, but individual servicemen chosen by me for the bellicose positions in which they had been cast. On the last Christmas day of pre-war peace, I received a clockwork train. It was later the cause of great amusement to my more opulent friends for it had only four wheels and no bogey. But it was loved by me not least because of its bright green LNER livery. It pulled four coal trucks and a guard's van around a tight circle of slightly warped line, passing on its way a signal box and a replica of the high water cisterns which were used to fill the boilers of steam-driven locomotives. My little toy – like the massive red cisterns on which it was modelled – worked on the simple gravity principle and consisted of no more than a tank and a tube. Unfortunately clockwork trains have no need of water. The result was regular patches of damp on the carpet and constant friction between my mother and me.

Nigel Hawthorne CBE
ACTOR

The puny waves broke suddenly and raced up the steep incline to trickle back as the next wave climbed and collided. He sat alone on the shingle wincing as the cold reached his toes, noticing the sag of tummy over his costume, aware of the crop of small white hairs pushing between the spread of freckles on the back of his hand. Remembering the thrill as the gigantic waves thundered in and skinny limbs scampered away at speed. And the squealing and the jumping up and down in puddles. And the salty tears while being dragged back to the Austin and dumped unceremoniously onto the hot seat where it had been in the sun.

James Herriot OBE, FRCVS

VETERINARY SURGEON AND AUTHOR

I went to a good school and received an excellent education but corporal punishment was popular in those days and all misdemeanours were rewarded with a few strokes of the 'tawse', the leather belt which was used in Scottish schools.

Since I had the unfortunate habit of laughing in class I was a regular recipient of the tawse, but I never really minded, because I could understand that it must have been irritating to the teachers to have me giggling during their serious attempts to impart learning. There was one subject which was a blind spot for me – mathematics. I was hopeless and on one occasion I distinguished myself by gaining a five per cent mark in a trigonometry exam.

Shortly after this my maths teacher called me out to the front of the class and informed me that he was going to give me six strokes of the belt. When I asked him what this was for he replied, 'Herriot, I have always thought you were just an amiable idiot and have treated you accordingly, but now I see that you have come out top of the class in your English paper, so I can only conclude that you have not been trying for me. Hold out your hand.'

He was wrong. I really was, and am, completely thick at maths and even now I have not the faintest notion what tangents, sines and cosines are all about.

I never minded all the beltings I received throughout my schooldays, but that was one time it really rankled.

Rachel Heyhoe Flint MBE

My first brush with the police taught me that, years ago, men had little regard for women cricketers, and my immediate instinct was to register protest. It happened early in my childhood – I think I was eight years old – while I was engaged in my customary tomboy habit of playing cricket with my brother Nicholas and his friends.

The road where I grew up was in a quiet suburb of Wolverhampton, and as there was so little traffic, the road became our sports arena. While the girls of the neighbourhood tended their dolls and prams, I preferred to play bicycle polo – a fraught, high-speed version of the royals' game – and soccer and cricket with the lads.

On this infamous occasion when I brushed with the law, we were some way through an intense cricket match in the road, when one of the local bobbies drove up. He marched towards us as we rushed for cover: aware that our games were at least frowned upon, if not illegal, we scattered to hiding-places behind various trees and hedges. The arm of the law yanked us all out one by one, however, and then out came the black notebook and pencil. He took the names and addresses of all the boys and then went to replace his notebook in his pocket. This was too much for me. I reached up, tapped him on the shoulder and pointed out that I had been playing cricket, too. His answer was most pitying. 'Girls don't play cricket,' which was about as devastating a blow to my pride as anyone could have delivered.

David Hicks

INTERIOR DESIGNER AND AUTHOR

When I was about thirteen my mother was sold a beautiful grey gelding called Nobby and with great pride I rode him over to the first East Essex Pony Club Gymkhana. As I arrived a fierce, plain, horsey woman stormed up to me saying 'What on earth are *you* doing on Greyling? He was stolen.' As I was alone it was acutely embarrassing. However, later on, money was refunded all round and paying rather more he became properly mine – and on Nobby I went on to win a cup for jumping.

Pamela Hicks

When I was ten years old, we were living in a house by the Sussex downs, not too far from Portsmouth, which was important for my father, being a naval officer. One day he was on 'stand-by' to rejoin his ship, but he thought he had a good chance of being able to have a last ride with my sister and me before going back to sea. In case the telephone call came, which was to summon him back to Portsmouth, he decided to take one of us at a time, leaving the other behind to gallop after him with the message.

He took me out with him first, my more responsible, elder sister being left to wait for the call. We had a good ride but I could not help hoping that the telephone call would not come until we returned to the house and it was my turn to wait and act as despatch rider. I could hardly believe my luck when we did get back before the call came.

I watched my sister and my father set off on their horses and I settled down to wait in the stableyard, holding my pony ready. After about half-an-hour the butler came hurrying out of the house and I saw him cross the yard and start talking urgently to the chauffeur and the head groom. I rushed over to them. 'Has the telephone call come?' I asked excitedly. 'Yes, Miss Pamela, but I am telling Mr Birch that he must saddle a horse and ride after his lordship. You are much too young to go off alone.' I could have cried with vexation. Frank Randall had been with my parents since they married and fussed over me like an old hen. 'But I am supposed to go. That's why I am waiting here.' The head groom came to my rescue. 'Miss Pamela will be all right and she will get there far quicker than I could.'

I did not wait to hear another word. I jumped on Puck, a little cream-coloured Welsh pony. Off we galloped through the woods, swerving around corners, chasing through the ferns, which grew higher than the pony and which my father called 'elephant's grass', and out onto the downs. Then a long gallop up hill, narrowly avoiding the treacherous rabbit holes, to where I could see my father and sister in the distance.

The moment they saw me they galloped up and we all raced towards home. They soon left little Puck and me panting far behind. But we returned triumphant and I have never forgotten the excitement of that ride.

Jimmy Hill
SPORTS COMMENTATOR

Although I didn't turn out to be a county cricketer, I will always be enormously grateful to a master at Cavendish Road Primary School, Balham for his enthusiasm for the game. His name was Garnham, and he devoted countless hours after school in the playground teaching us the fundamentals of the game of cricket. It didn't seem necessary in football; we played instinctively and constantly practised our skills with tennis balls in playground and street. Cricket was different: it required the correct techniques to be learned and applied in order to create a solid foundation of performance with bat and ball.

To start with, we were taught painstakingly to hold the bat properly; to play straight down the line, to use our feet to play forward or back when appropriate. It all sounds so simple now and obvious, but what a wonderful opportunity, for a lifetime's pleasure was being nurtured. So many young players grow up now with a good eye and appalling technique, because the Mr Garnhams of this world seem to have largely disappeared and only the fortunate few are blessed with such valuable guidance at the time when it matters. It was simplicity itself; a small flat disc was placed on all the playground wickets on a length to encourage accuracy. When I hear the commentators recommending line and length to bowlers of test calibre, I know that Mr Garnham would be approving.

One particular debt of gratitude I owe him was in relation to the award of a Hobbs bat at the age of just eight for scoring 31 not out against much older boys. The early days of sponsorship and marketing linked the *Star* newspaper and that incomparable batsman, Jack Hobbs with an award scheme for schoolboys. I don't suppose any other trophy could have meant quite as much at any time in my life. I'm afraid the bat has long since vanished, but not my gratitude to our Mr Garnham for inspiring the winning of it. Sadly, such people have become almost extinct; not entirely, I'm glad to say, in tribute to those who still care and pass on their knowledge to young hopefuls. We are told our lifestyle is better than ever these days. Not in one respect, no one could have cared more about cricket and his pupils than my teacher of old, which is why I remember him so clearly.

Above: Jeremy Irons as a young boy
Below left: Gordon Honeycombe with his
mother in Karachi, then in British India
Below right: Sally Jones, as a Brownie
aged seven

Above: H.R.F. Keating (right) with his
father and younger brother
Below: Jeremy Kemp at school in 1941,
aged seven

Above: Diana Lamplugh with Whitle

Sir Peter Holmes MC

CHAIRMAN OF SHELL TRANSPORT AND TRADING PLC

Eileen 'M' was the only other English child in our neighbourhood. So inevitably we became fast friends, playing together nearly every day for four years; the years that we were four, five, six and seven. We played all the games that children play – from dolls' houses to throwing stones at a tree full of chestnuts. Then the war came.

We grew up in Budapest, high on a hill above the Danube. But in August 1939 it was time for the English to leave. So our two mothers led our elder brothers (one each) and Eileen and me on a trek across southern Europe to Venice, to catch a train to Paris. The journey was a great adventure. Eileen and I each carried a very small suitcase full of very precious things; precious to us, aged seven, that is.

Our train was supposed to be the last train that would run before war broke out, so it was with much chagrin on the part of the grown-ups that after several days travel we missed the train by five minutes. (Indeed I had never seen grown-ups cry, before, and this so impressed me that I immediately caught 'stationitis' for life – this is a disease which ensures I am absurdly early if I have to catch a train.)

In fact this was not the last train, and we found ourselves back in Dover a few days later. There our families went our separate ways, and as time went by Eileen became a distant childhood memory.

The years passed. School, the army, university, three decades of work and life abroad. And then, in 1984, I was asked to join the Council of a distinguished London Society. I noticed on the letterhead that the Administration Director of the Society was an Eileen 'M'. It was a long shot, but as I walked into my first Council meeting I asked this lady if she had by any chance grown up in Budapest. 'You're Peter, aren't you?', the Eileen of my childhood replied.

My wife tells me that Eileen and I talk together as if we had been separated for forty-five minutes, not forty-five years.

Childhood Memories

Bob Holness
TELEVISION AND RADIO PRESENTER

One of my very earliest memories concerns Christmas and Santa Claus.

We lived in Herne Bay, Kent, and my parents had decided to move house. I was very excited, but then extremely worried when I found that – unlike our old house – the new one was a bungalow with electric fires . . . and NO chimney! How was Santa Claus going to get in to leave my presents? My parents said I wasn't to worry, as he had a way of doing these things . . . but that didn't satisfy me. I waited until everyone was asleep and then I opened my bedroom window as wide as it would go . . . and propped the door open, so that the presents could be left under the tree in the living-room.

It was the coldest night's sleep I can ever remember, with a smattering of snow when I woke. My folks were furious, saying I could have caught a very bad chill . . . but I pointed out that it was all worth while as he HAD found his way: he'd left me a train set!! And – happily – the threatened cold never came.

Gordon Honeycombe
TELEVISION NEWSREADER AND AUTHOR

I remember being in a pram, a high pram, and being very hot. I think this was because my *ayah* – I was born in Karachi, then in British India – had left me too long in the sun. We lived in Bath Island Road, in a large first floor flat in a mansion called Variawa House. It had tiled floors and punkahs, and the four of us had three full-time servants. My father worked for an American oil company, Standard Vac, as a sales manager.

I remember my father had a cine-camera, and at every birthday or Christmas party in our home, we children would bunch on the sitting-room carpet and gaze entranced at the silent black and white pictures on the silvered screen, while the reels in the flickering projector rattled and unrolled. There were Laurel and Hardy, Mickey Mouse and Donald Duck, and my favourite, Charlie Chaplin. Even now, when I see scenes from *The Cure* and *The Gold Rush*, that childish glee is recaptured.

66

I also remember the magic of the movies, and being en-thralled in a dark and stuffy cinema by the first showing of *Snow White and the Seven Dwarfs*, *Bambi*, *The Wizard of Oz*, *Beyond the Blue Horizon*; and war films like *Eagle Squadron*, *Wake Island* and *Mrs Miniver*. My mother suggested at the interval of *Gone with the Wind* that we could go home – the film was over three hours long. 'You can go, if you like,' I replied. 'I'm staying.' Music also seized my imagination, whether heard on the wireless, on the gramophone, or in the films I saw. For some reason 'The Anniversary Waltz', sung by Bing Crosby, and 'Jealousy', impinged most on my memory, and for more obvious reasons, 'White Christmas'. I had never seen snow.

I don't remember rain or that it ever rained, though it must have happened in the monsoon season. The sun always seems to be shining in my childhood. Sometimes there were dust-storms, and the heat was sometimes uncomfortable. For I was an anaemic child, thin and pale. There was a war, but it was somewhere else. Some men in khaki uniforms came to the house, or were seen socially. But they were fun: they had presents for children, especially the Americans – chewing-gum and candy. We collected tin cans and bottle-tops for what was called a War Effort. But it was so much of an effort that we soon desisted, concentrating on childish pleasures.

Parties, for adults as well as for children, seemed to be frequent, and often involved fancy dress. Certainly the adults enjoyed themselves as much as their offspring, especially at the various clubs, where at weekends we children would gather and run about, between bouts of drinking lemonade and munching peanuts. There was the Gymkhana, the Boat Club, the Golf Club and the Sind Club, though the latter was not a place for play. I never met an Indian who wasn't a servant or served the Sahib and Mem-sahib in some capacity, and a Chota-(Small)-Sahib like me.

These were the last years of the Raj, and the British were making the most of it, marooned in India by the War and having a jolly good time. Soon enough the Westerners' sun would set, and the cold east wind of Edinburgh, the drabness and rationing of post-war Scotland, would freeze my skinny body and blight my trustful soul, as would school regimes and organized games. My wide-eyed innocence slowly corroded. It had survived all but untarnished in India, where nothing that happened was right or wrong, only different from yesterday's novelties.

Sir Michael Hordern CBE

ACTOR

My First Fish

As if it were yesterday I vividly remember the event on the Grand Union Canal at Berkhampsted, where I had been born four and a half years before. I remember the clumps of rushes on the water's edge, I remember the little red float bobbing and disappearing, my elder brother's shout and the little fingerling roach flickering through the air and on to the bank.

I remember bitterly the tears that I shed when my brother – a grown-up young man of nine – made me put it back because it was too small, when all I wanted to do was to take it proudly home to show Mummy.

My brother is now eighty-two but I still go fishing with him and quite frequently I am allowed to take the fish home.

Gloria Hunniford

RADIO AND TELEVISION PRESENTER

When I was about five years old, my mother tells me I was found looking up in a rather intrigued way at a friend of hers. They had met in the main shopping area and were having a chat, when suddenly I said 'Oh, your nose is just as big as everyone says.' Almost the end of a friendship!!!

Jeremy Irons

ACTOR, DIRECTOR AND FATHER

My first conscious memory is of lying in my pram one sunny morning in our gently sloping garden in St Helens, Isle of Wight and like most children of pram age I suspect I was a jiggler. In any case, some untoward movement caused the brake of the pram to fail in its function and the pram began to move slowly at first, but gaining speed all the time, down the garden away from the house. I suspect I must have let out an involuntary cry for I remember my mother appearing through the wattled gate, which closed off the kitchen yard, holding a wooden spoon in her hand and at that moment, or shortly afterwards, the pram tipped and I found myself lying among the marrow patch. A fortunate destination since the largeness of the leaves cushioned my fall and being the size I was a large green marrow, rather than being a threat, is somewhat of a comfort – a similar-sized body!

Sally Jones

BBC SPORTS PRESENTER, JOURNALIST AND AUTHOR

My First School

As a child, I was brought up in the Staffordshire countryside near Burton-on-Trent and went to Bretby village school. It was an old-fashioned place; a Victorian school-house divided into two rooms with high ceilings, whitewashed brick walls, battered desks and slippery wooden floors smelling of wax polish. Twenty-four children aged from four to eleven trekked there from miles around along narrow lanes, the children of farm labourers and bank clerks, scientists and grave-diggers.

Miss Spencer, all dark curls and a spot of red on each cheek like a Dutch doll took the lower form. She was kind, undemanding and smelled of flowers, smiling vaguely while we locked each other out of the Wendy house or measured out scoops of sand from the sandpit on the scales, then tipped it over our friends' heads.

Any child considered capable of holding its own in the rough and tumble of 'top-class' was at once moved up, regardless of age into the big room over which Miss Hindson presided, small and imperious in mauve silk and heavy Victorian brooches. With her aquiline nose and fierce dark eyes, she at first seemed a formidable figure, ramrod straight behind an enormous desk with her little dog Shandy at her feet. Like his mistress, Shandy had a short fuse but a bark that was far worse than his bite. He also regarded the space beneath the desk as his private property and the more daring of us would secretly thrust our feet into his lair as we queued up with our dinner-money, in order to make him growl bloodcurdlingly.

Few took such liberties with Miss Hindson who was neverthe-less an unorthodox but inspiring teacher. With none of the modern prejudices against rote-learning, she would set us chanting our tables, memorizing the exciting bits of Kipling or Tennyson or scribbling away at table-tests until even the stupidest could multiply at the speed of light and give a tolerable rendering of 'The Charge of the Light Brigade' or 'How Horatio Kept the Bridge'. More than twenty years later, most still can.

It was an old-fashioned school and although modern educa-tionalists would doubtless throw up their hands in horror at its illiberality, it taught the traditional values of competition, hard work and self-discipline in a way that caught our imaginations and powerfully affected our lives.

H.R.F. Keating

CRIME NOVELIST

It was, I think, when I was aged eight, or perhaps nine. And it led to a career as a writer of crime fiction.

I had been brought up, as all good children were in those golden days shortly before the Second World War, to believe it was 'a sin to tell a lie'. But one summer day – summer lasted then, with one short interval for Christmas, from one year's end to another – I was out with my father and an uncle in the car, and my father, chatting away, shot a red light right under the eye of a passing policeman. He was gravely spoken to.

Then when we arrived home it was tea-time, a marked point in every single day in that halcyon era, and we sat under the big cherry tree to have it. My father then recounted to my mother what had happened. And, to my amazement, it was not what I had seen happen and what my father, talking with my uncle on the way home, had spoken of as having happened. Now, mysteriously, that minor infringement of the traffic law was not at all my father's fault. A lie had been told. Uttered by God. At at least by my god.

And from the obsession with the matter of lying that grew with me from that moment on there came, one day some twenty years later, the realization that a detective novel – my first effort had just been published – could do more than set a little puzzle. It could be used to talk of things that affect people. Like lies. Books like that were worth devoting all one's life to.

Jeremy Kemp

ACTOR

Doctor Davis

In the early autumn of 1939 people of all sizes in Britain were being exhorted to – among other things – 'Put Out More Flags'. I personally spent much of this time staying with my paternal grandparents who lived in a pretty remote part of the North Riding of Yorkshire. This area was thought to be safe. I was very busy in the pursuit of the war effort. The collection from the hedgerows of various items, especially 'hips and haws', was considered important and could be undertaken by small persons. My grandmother saw to it that it was.

I was not yet five years old. Figures like Neville Chamberlain and indeed Adolf Hitler were much less familiar to me than for example Mrs Dawson, the cook, or Foreman, the gamekeeper – the latter always armed anyway and presumably quite capable of seeing off any Germans. One somehow felt that Foreman and his twelve-bore would be a match for any serious opposition. Guns were used in my world for murdering the garden rabbit – often unsuccessfully – also for assaulting a variety of other creatures including pheasants, grouse, partridge, woodcock. A Panzer Division had little meaning. Foreman striding through the early morning mist, clad in boots, breeches, leggings, cap and bearing a twelve-bore most certainly did.

As soon as one 'descended' from the hills to the flat part, i.e. the Vale of York, the RAF was everywhere – Topcliffe, Dishforth, Leeming Bar. I very seldom 'descended'. It was too far to walk or really to bicycle. There was no public transport. Petrol of course was a peculiar colour and very much rationed. I seem to remember accompanying my grandmother to something called the 'Salvation Army', almost certainly to do with my behaviour. Much tea and many buns were distributed to many soldiers. I was severely reprimanded for failing to recognize or behave appropriately before the Princess Royal. She lived nearby at Harewood. I never went again.

It was the night time which brought the real excitement. At this time the various aircraft would take off, and we hoped, of course, land again, having accomplished what they had set off to do. There were many searchlights piercing the sky. I went to bed as I remember around 6 o'clock. But many nights I did not sleep until the Lancasters returned from whence they had so secretly been. 'Son et Lumière' – and free. My grandparents' house had no mains electricity so there was nothing to interrupt my view. It was almost certainly this lack of sleep which caused pasty-facedness, great bags under the eyes, general debilitation and subsequently much daydreaming while supposedly mastering the seven-times table. These symptoms were diagnosed by my grandmother as certainly caused by bad manners, bad behaviour and poor sleeping. I was at this time obliged to sleep in a ghastly kind of 'scrumcap' affair – not because my ears stuck out but lest they might. Anyway the Doctor was sent for.

What a stroke of luck. The doctor was very good news. He arrived by car – an excitement in itself – and sometimes dressed for hunting. Normally, he was very tweedy, smelt of horses, I think, very kind and told lots of jokes, many of which made me laugh quite a lot. Most important of all, he always carried, secreted about his person a number of Barleysugars. The first and main part of the examination was always a Barleysugar hunt. Where could they be? He had so many pockets.

Also he was not unknown to cheat a little. Deftly popping a sweetie into a pocket which you had already searched. He thoroughly enjoyed this form of consultation himself. But the main purpose of this process was designed to persuade my grandmother that much serious 'doctoring' was going on.

After about three sweeties had been located and triumphantly pocketed (sweets like petrol were heavily rationed and thus even more desirable) my grandmother was sent for. She would appear looking very severe and clearly hoping for 'disgusting medicine' to be prescribed. 'Well?' she would ask 'Nothing to worry about, Violet, old girl – nothing to worry about at all . . . PURE WICKEDNESS I should say'. At the same time winking at me so obviously that I felt sure the game was up. This diagnosis was of course in general accordance with my grandmother's theories. She had much to do with wickedness, she played the organ in the church and the Archbishop of York came occasionally to tea.

Some form of punishment was usually administered, quite unjustly. But I did not complain. A visit from Dr Davis was a most desirable event and I would begin at once to work upon contriving another. 'Pure Wickedness' was never all bad.

Miles Kington

JOURNALIST

Learning to Dance

Dancing lessons. I had forgotten all about those. But, yes, my first boarding school took dancing very seriously and insisted that we learn the rudiments of the waltz, the quick-step and the samba – the samba was very popular just then. I hated the whole business: I could see an idle fascination in the way the steps fitted to the music, and the geometry of the waltz quite interested me, but I didn't see the point of actually *doing* it. Especially doing it with other boys. It being an all-male school, we had to solemnly take little boys in shorts in our arms and pretend they were partners at the big ball, and every time I met a woman who has terrible memories of 'leading' as a man in dancing lessons, they seem surprised to learn that I have suffered the opposite indignity. The only thing worse than having to take a 'female' partner in your arms was being embraced by your 'male' partner.

I had forgotten all about the swapping that goes on at school. They also took boxing very seriously, and our instructor, a tough Glaswegian named Cruickshank, took it even more seriously than the school. One day he told us to get into pairs, and I paired off with my best friend. Then he told us to start boxing, one defending, the other attacking. My best friend was a good deal tougher than me, so I asked him to defend while I ineffectually attacked. Fine. Then the instructor yelled: 'Swap round!' and for three minutes my best friend beat the living daylights out of me, while I vainly tried to defend myself. He ceased to be my best or any kind of friend at that moment.

Sometimes they imported girls from a nearby school for dancing, and they pretended to be female partners instead. They were better, but not a lot, as half of them were used to dancing the male role and stepped on your toes a lot. And there was always something rather incongruous about pre-pubertal children dancing together. It was as artificial as going on holiday together or writing letters to each other. I must have confessed something of the sort to my father, because he became worried and ordained private dancing lessons for me and my brother during the holidays. Dear reader, did you have a father who was

73

worried about your attainments? I did, and I'm glad I did in a way, because it got me into playing the piano, and golf, and one or two other things I quite enjoyed, but *private dancing lessons*? My brother and I stood in this dance studio in North Wales and waited our turn to be whirled round by Mrs Instructress, all alone the three of us, like a scene from some film on Channel 4 with French subtitles. The only respite came when she went to change the music. I hated it, and I never got any better.

My father, who had been a superb dancer, and still was compared to his children, was upset by this, as he saw dancing as an important social asset. In later life, many an elderly lady has said to me with dreamy eyes, 'My God, how your father could dance – it was magic in his arms'. He could still do a passable charleston at the age of sixty, when I couldn't do a passable anything. I think he even began to suspect after a while that it wasn't dancing I didn't like: it was girls. This was absolute nonsense. I thought girls were wonderful, so wonderful that I didn't even dare speak to them, largely brought on by my having been sent away to boarding school by the very same father of whom I speak. I spent most of my teens trying to listen to, and play, jazz, which was my ruling passion and probably still is.

Give my father his due, he introduced me some time later to someone who ran the local dance band which played at the Wrexham Memorial Hall on a Saturday night. They played for dancing, but they also played a lot of jazz, and as a teenage second trombonist I was in seventh heaven. I was playing in a band, playing jazz, and *not having to dance*. I had finally stumbled on the great truth: there are some people who like to play and some who like to dance, and the two categories never overlap, or rarely enough to matter. I have made a point of asking musicians down the years whether they like dancing and scarcely found a dozen who did.

Nobody in the Wrexham band danced. They stared down from the stage at the sheeplike dancers on the floor and it was with contempt that they stared – or perhaps indifference, because contempt suggests a lively interest. A musician's attitude to music was: if it is bad, who would want to dance to it? If it was good, listen to it. The trumpeter, Reg, used to amuse himself by watching out for dancing couples who clung too close together or embraced hotly, and when they passed in front of the bandstand he would make loud kissing noises through his instrument. Guiltily they would spring apart and look round.

Mock-strictly, he would shake his finger at them. Ah, it was great in that band for a young lad, having a wee drop at half time and hearing my first musician's dirty stories.

One day I was asked to dance by the saxophonist's wife, who was extremely attractive and vivacious. Halfway through our second dance she suddenly ignored my splayed feet and nervous actions, and plunged me into the hottest kiss I had ever undergone, if indeed I had ever undergone one before. I was bowled over. Suddenly dancing took on a new light. But I was also horrified and tore myself away, saying: 'What if Malcolm sees you?'

'Malcolm?' she said, looking back at the stand. 'When he plays music, he never sees anything but the music.'

And I was plunged into my steamy kiss again. Playing in the band was never quite the same thereafter, as I sensed there was a bigger world outside playing music and talking musicians' talk. The fact that it might involve dancing from time to time seemed to be a chance I would have to take, and an ordeal I would have to suffer.

Sheila Kitzinger MBE

AUTHOR, BIRTH EDUCATOR AND SOCIAL ANTHROPOLOGIST

In many large families in the past the nursery seems to have had a life of its own. Children got up to all sorts of secret adventures hidden from the eyes of grown-ups. Wonderful stories like Nurse Matilda, which delighted my own children, recount the antics of families of naughty children who outdo each other in imaginative invention. Children, it seems, weren't exposed to the constant searchlight of careful rearing. Their anxious parents weren't constantly scanning them for signs of progress or trying out different theories of parent-child interaction in order to encourage pyscho-social development or intellectual ability. Instead, children could relax and be children, flourishing like wild flowers.

I was a child in a small family – just my brother David (two years younger) and me. We grew up in the 1930s and 1940s. Mother read radical books about child psychology and was convinced of the value of the educational theories of Bertrand

Russell, A.S. Neil and Maria Montessori. The result was a carefully constructed mix and match of educational principles with strong emphasis on openness and thinking, creativity and the excitement of learning – for which I shall always be grateful.

We were carefully nurtured nearly all the time. But after dark we were free to have adventures. We lived in an ugly, rambling Victorian house in a nondescript street close to the station in a Somerset market town. Our rooms were at the top in what had once been attics. At night, and especially in moonlight, they were the starting point of elicit expeditions out of David's window and across the red-tiled roof, along the gables – balancing carefully, and onto the next roof at right angles to it, followed by a jump across a gulf to the garage roofs adjoining.

It was another world out there – the air often chilly and crisp, sometimes mothy and warm, darkness enveloping the squat ordinariness of the yard below, the dog kennel in which Toby lay crouched, nose sniffing, the bitter-smelling laurel bushes, the spiky iron gates, and the crude angles of all these objects which seemed to me the ugliest things in the world.

Climbing out of the window, we first crept on all-fours, one in front of the other. Then we stood, balancing precariously on the roof top, arms extended and could see over the clustering roofs all the way to the station. There the signal lights glowed, shining pools of incandescent magic, in what seemed like caverns where monster trains waited, belching steam in the dark. A great grinding noise, followed by a huffing and puffing and dragging of mighty chains, and a train would shunt – the lights changed from red to green – and the monster snaked its way to another siding. Occasionally there was a ghostly whistle or a shrill scream. Trains clanked and trundled. Then the night express swept through without stopping, rectangles of light shooting past like a flipped pack of cards, cutting through the night like an earth-bound comet. After that there was an extraordinary stillness, as the station breathed itself back into mystery and the dragons started to grunt and groan and stir themselves again.

On the rooftops we experienced a private world where we could triumph over demons and monsters. That dangerous journey gave us precious things – a shared adventure, an intense sensory experience, a marvelling at mystery, the awareness that we usually see only from one angle and in only one light – and that there are other ways of seeing, and an exultant joy in our own power.

76

Diana Lamplugh

FOUNDER OF THE SUZY LAMPLUGH TRUST

'The Diary and the Blessing'

It was opening Whitle's diary that brought it all back. There it was – 1942 – the *real* story:

> Took Diana and Angela to church
> Slightly cloudy.
> Germany invaded . . .

Day after day, brief notes of mundane happenings of a rather peculiar family life, the weather, and a line at the bottom noting the daily horrendous happenings 'over there'.

The small book fell into my possession when I cleared up Whitle's 'home', a room in an Old People's Sanctuary for Retired Teachers. Her death occurred at the age of 102 which was a tremendous achievement helped by her determination to live until she acquired the best room in the place – 'I watched the coffin pass by my window' she told me with satisfaction as she surveyed her prize on my penultimate visit. After this she needed to strive no more and she let go of her life gracefully, gradually sinking into sleep.

Now, however, I felt as though she was alive again. Memories came flooding back, evoked by those clipped but evocative sentences. Whitle's real name, which she much despised, was Jessica White. She had been my mother's housemistress at The Cheltenham Ladies' College. When my mother graduated to Bedford P.E. College she retained the link and by the time my parents were married a fine bond of friendship was established.

When war broke out it seemed quite natural that Whitle should join our household. My recollection of our inaptly named house ('Caregwynt' meant Windy Rocks) was that it was enormous. In fact, it was not that big but we had many rooms and space was at a premium. Every place needed to be fully used as part of the 'War Effort'. My mother with Whitle decided to run a small boarding school for children whose parents were both involved with war work. My younger brother and I were joined by a fluctuating number of children around our own ages. As I read through the weeks, the months, in that diary I knew with certainty that those were times of great happiness.

77

We slept in dormitories; we had whooping cough together (imagine all those pans!); we romped in the light evenings of double summertime (my brother fell against the window and ended up with his bare posterior through the pane – I only remember our giggles not his pain); we aired our Liberty Bodices (why on earth did we have those?) on the guard round the gas fire; we hid together in the cubby hole under the stairs when there was an air raid (great fun for we were always rewarded with special treats – the adults eating even more than us. It must have been sparse rationed food but that did not impinge on our pleasure).

I suppose we should have felt deprived. My father was a mainly absent figure to whom we sent our first 'joined-up' writing' and from whom we received a weird object – a banana – which we ate in small pieces and wondered if we liked it. In reality my father, one of the Desert Rats, was badly injured at Dunkirk and became one of the secretaries in Churchill's 'Bunker' ('all reports needed short sentences, and if the person on the phone had a stutter it might well really be the K-K-King'). My mother must have often been distressed, worried, lonely and afraid. But I cannot dredge this picture up from my recollections at all.

Whitle was always there, standing beautifully upright, quick of tongue, demanding perfection while helping us to achieve it; she was a stickler for the truth. Whitle taught us to love the English language (my first visit to the theatre was when she took me to see *A Midsummer Night's Dream* and it sealed my delight in the spoken word). She taught us to knit and sew (boys as well as girls – 'It's just as essential for everyone'). She delighted in flowers and long walks (a healthy life was instilled in our subconscious). Whitle nursed us through ailments without any sentimental touches; we were just expected to get better (she soothed my brother's asthma as if by magic). Our lives were dynamic, full of interest and yet permeated by calm.

Looking back, I can sense no fear, no foreboding, no horrors. We were privileged for we had that ingredient which often seems to be missing these days in family life – a one hundred per cent supporter. A maiden lady who considered all her charges to be her family; a lady without means who had some of the greatest wealth of all, an amazing capacity for living. A lady who had no degrees or honours and yet was one of the most learned I have ever met. A lady who had no self pity or regrets.

After the war and for the rest of her life, she lived alongside our family, teaching even our dyslexic children to read. Though her bones became brittle, her intellect never faltered. Her eyes dimmed but she continued to revel in the radio, not only listening to drama but also to the world and national news. Her perceptions were mischieviously acute, her sense of humour was wicked. We would still discuss politics and the latest trends right up until her hundredth birthday.

We flew back from our twenty-fifth wedding anniversary honeymoon especially for that party. None of us would have dreamed of missing that occasion. It was a celebration for a Great Lady; Earl Spencer, the Princess of Wales' father, came and planted a rose bush in her honour. The other ladies made a beautiful pressed flower calendar. We drank a toast to the lady who gave us stability, a sense of duty and purpose.

Whitle enriched many a childhood.

Peter Lee

CLAIRVOYANT

One of my early childhood memories was my first public appearance on a stage. It was during a 'Victory over Europe' children's celebration street party and I was four years of age when I won first prize in the talent contest by singing a road safety song, made famous when Gracie Fields recorded it at a children's hospital. I do believe the hospital was Great Ormond Street. I still remember some of the words. Let me sing them to you.

> Listen all you children, I've a tale to tell
> All you little girls and little boys as well
> When you leave the school room
> When you are at your play
> Don't run into danger, listen to what I say
> If you cross the road by day or night
> Beware of the danger that looms in sight.
> Look to the left and look to the right and you'll
> NEVER EVER GET RUN OVER

Childhood Memories

Rustie Lee
TELEVISION PERSONALITY AND COMEDIENNE

One of my earliest and loveliest memories is as a small child living with my grandmother in Jamaica after my parents had left to make a home for us in England. 'Momadada', as I called my grandmother, lived high on the hills in the countryside above Hope Bay and had a beautifully clear-flowing stream running through her vegetable garden. Us children used to spend many happy hours paddling in the stream and catching the translucent shrimps in our home-made nets which we took back for grandma to cook for tea. Happy, sunny childhood days – is it a wonder that we never forget them?

Bernard Levin
JOURNALIST

I cannot remember when and how I began to look at pictures. This in itself strikes me as odd. I can remember very clearly my first steps into music, including the false ones, just as I can recall the details of my early reading, and of my first responses to landscape (though that last is easy, because my first *sight* of landscape, let alone response to it, was so late) and the theatre. But peer as I may into the darkness, I can see no clue – who, what, where – to the awakening of an interest in the visual arts.

This suggests that it must have taken place before I was nine, before the amnesiac curtain rises, but that cannot be true; there was no one in my home with any knowledge of pictures, no one, indeed, who would so much as have heard of the National Gallery. Nor was there anything I can remember on the walls of my childhood home that had anything to do with art, with the exception of a curiously ugly silk-embroidered picture in the Chinese manner.

What the walls bore was a series of huge and gloomy family photographs, studio portraits, all of which I can see most clearly. Chief among them was one of my maternal grandparents, to which there was a mystery attached, with a comic explanation. The mystery lay in the fact that on one side of the couple the photograph merged into a smudgy *drawing* of an aspidistra,

Above: Martyn Lewis on his tricycle
Right: Maureen Lipman
Below: The Earl of Lichfield with the family chauffeur

Above: Hayley Mills with her dog Hamlet
Left: John Motson enjoying a seaside holiday in Lincolnshire
Below: Derek Nimmo as a young boy

Above: John Julius Norwich, aged four
Right: Charles Osborne with his mother in Brisbane, Australia
Below: The Rt. Hon. Dr David Owen MP (centre, middle row) at prep school

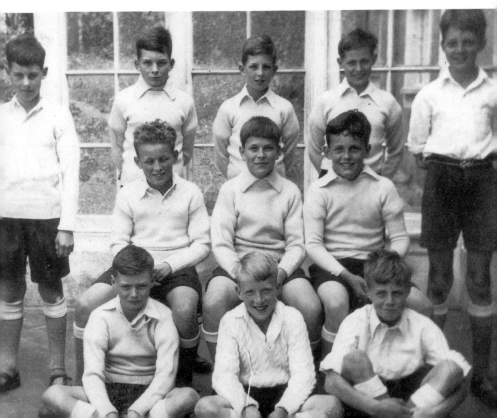

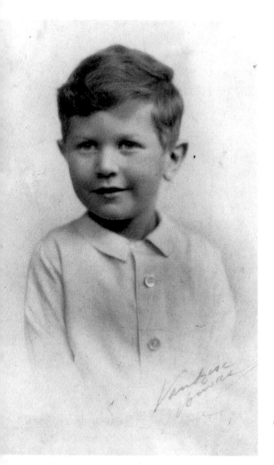

Above left: The Rt. Hon. Lord Prior, aged four
Above right: Nicholas Parsons aged four
Left: A painting by Jan Pieńkowski aged eight to illustrate the fairy story of the Fern Flower, a story from his native Czechoslovakia

and on the other into an equally unconvincing pillar. The explanation was that my grandparents had posed with their two eldest children, my mother and one of her brothers, but that they had made faces at the camera and had to be expunged into disgrace. My most vivid memory of the explanation lies in the shock I had (I can still feel it) at the discovery that my mother had been naughty. I found it impossible to attach the concept to her, or indeed to envisage her as a child at all.

My grandfather had been a handsome man: when I first knew him he looked a little like Stalin, and something of the resemblance lasted, but in that picture there was nothing either patriarchal or authoritative, just a gentle paterfamilias with a wife who already bore the signs of the shrew in the line between her brows. Still, she also bore one of the world's most beautiful names: Bathsheba.

The next photograph was of my mother, grown up now and no longer making faces at the camera. Oddly, the picture as I remember it made her look bigger than reality, for she was a diminutive woman throughout her life. She looked rather like her mother in the photograph, but the resemblance must have faded quickly, because I could never see it even as a child, though they were both always before me for comparison. My three uncles followed, one of whom, Mark, I never knew, for he had been killed in the Great War, long before I was born. There was a curious phrase attached to mention of him and his death, the meaning of which I did not discover till decades later: Lord Derby's Scheme. (It was a form of enlistment somewhere between volunteering and conscription.) My mother told me many years later that my grandparents had journeyed after the war to see his grave in Flanders, the only time either of them had left Britain since they arrived here from the Pale at the turn of the century (nor did they ever leave again); they found his headstone marked with a cross, and got it changed to a Star of David. Mention of Uncle Mark in my grandparents' presence was forbidden, as it would inevitably produce tears; the same was true, much more intensely, after my mother's only sister, youngest of the family, whose photograph completed the set, died soon after I went away to school. She suffered from asthma, and the house was often full of the curious sweet smell of the medicinal joss-sticks that were supposed to give her relief.

It was much more likely, though I did not realize it at the time, that she was suffering from the same sort of malady as that which afflicted Elizabeth Barrett – boredom and a feeling of aimlessness – but with no Robert Browning to pluck her from the chaise-longue. (I have only just realized, in the course of writing this paragraph, that my grandparents must have had a lucky escape after the Second World War; they were never naturalized, and could easily have been among those Russians who had been settled in Britain since long before the Soviet Union existed, but were nevertheless enthusiastically sent to Russia by the Foreign Office to be exterminated in Stalin's death-camps.)

Martyn Lewis

TELEVISION NEWSREADER

Childhood for me is a host of conflicting memories – I remember being kitted out in a blue mackintosh several sizes too big because my mother thought I should 'grow into it', and being mercilessly ribbed because in an era of kneelength trench-coats it came down to my ankles. There was the bright blue and silver tricycle – my first – which my father rescued from the scrap heap and lovingly rebuilt and repainted until it looked like new. Outgrowing it was a great regret. There was the primitive spear I made out of a piece of bamboo and a shaped six-inch nail, which I used to catch my very first flat-fish. I proudly brought it home for my mother to fillet and cook – and was extremely disappointed when it turned out to be two tiny tasteless mouthfuls.

There was the rehearsal for the school play – *Henry IV Part I* – when I was playing Prince Hal, and a sword fight left me with a nine-inch scrape on my arm as Hotspur's sword went a touch too far. And talking of scrapes, school trips provided more than their fair share of those: the brakes on a bus failed going down a winding mountain road – we ended up hanging over a steep slope, with everyone having to move gingerly to the back of the bus to stop it toppling down the mountainside. On an expedition up Ireland's highest mountain – Errigal in County Donegal – an orange I had just peeled slipped out of my grasp, and my instinctive reaction was to lean over to try to catch it. Luckily a watchful Latin master grabbed my arm and saved me from a two-hundred-foot sheer drop. I think it was on the same school camp that my tent burned down around me while I slept – I woke up to find my life saved by the canvas sleeping-bag cover my mother had used in the evacuation of Dunkirk, and which she had insisted on me taking on the trip despite my loud protests. On a lighter side, I remember moving briefly, at the age of eleven, to a school where I was extremely unhappy, so much so that I developed an appalling stutter which lasted several months, ending only after I returned to my old school.

The Rt. Hon. the Earl of Lichfield
FBIPP, FRPS
PHOTOGRAPHER

From a School Report

By the time this boy learns to speak French he'll be too old to cross the Channel.

Maureen Lipman
ACTRESS AND AUTHOR

From a School Report, Spring 1961, Newland High School for Girls, aged fourteen

'Maureen still does not take criticism with a very good grace'.

How true those words were. Even today among all the plaudits it's still the carping ones which come back into my head – usually in performance! I also note that the word 'silliness' was used five times in one report and I'm thrilled to feel I've grown up to make a career out of it.

The Rt. Hon. the Earl of Longford KG

My father, a retired soldier, used to take me for long walks before the First World War. I used to pester him with questions: 'Is Lloyd George a good man?'; 'Is Kitchener a good general?'; 'Is George V a good king?' One day he broke into this interrogation by suddenly remarking 'I'd give ten years of my life to take part in a charge'.

About a year later he was killed leading his brigade at Gallipoli. He had commanded the Second Lifeguards so he might have preferred a cavalry charge but an infantry charge probably deprived him of thirty years of life. He was fifty-one, rather more than thirty years younger than I am now and he was much fitter.

Charles McCall ROI, NEAC

ARTIST

Memories of an Edwardian Childhood

My childhood was at the end of the Edwardian era. The special treats were summer days on the beaches near Edinburgh with my Aunts Bella, Hannah, Jean and Liz. Aunt Liz was the eldest and my favourite, always thrusting presents in my hands, with a finger on her lips as a signal to keep silent.

They all wore long sweeping dresses, which made lovely patterns on the sand as they walked. It was a great surprise to me at the end of the First World War, when suddenly one realized women had legs!

I knew right away I had to be an artist. I sketched everything. At school I drew the generals of the war, and gave them to schoolfriends for sweets. I was not Scottish for nothing! My grandfather had been an artist, but died young, leaving my grandmother with a son and four daughters to educate. Grandmother was a fearsome old lady, always in black, and smelling faintly of mothballs. She had a large tabby cat called Punch. It amused my aunts when I announced that Punchie had grate stocking legs, and a grate stocking tail! (Meaning the bars of the fire.) I always loved cats, and mother and I had a cat called Snooks. We both cried bitterly when he died of rat poisoning.

As a boy I was very belligerent, and was in the middle of a fight with another boy, sitting on his chest and banging his head on the pavement, when a man came up and said 'Do you not know it is Armistice Day? There should be no more fighting after eleven o'clock'.

Mark H. McCormack
CHAIRMAN OF INTERNATIONAL MANAGEMENT GROUP

My godfather was a very famous American writer – Carl Sandburg – and when I was a very young boy, each 4th July we had a beach party near our summer home on Lake Michigan and at this party, Carl Sandburg would always tell me he was going to bring a bubble hat made of bubbles and yet he never once wore it to the beach party! I remember, as a very young boy, anticipating the arrival of the bubble hat. In 1936, Carl Sandburg wrote a poem about me titled 'Mark Waits In Anticipation' which appeared in *Good Housekeeping*, which dedicated itself to this particular memory.

Michael McCrum
MASTER OF CORPUS CHRISTI COLLEGE, CAMBRIDGE

A Dartmoor Experience

There they were; seven or eight of them, on the moorland sky line above me, tramping across the heather, looking like little men. It was a hot, sunny day, and, although I was about half a mile away below them in the valley, I could see enough of the strange style and bright colours of their clothes and hats to know for certain that *at last* I was looking at real Dartmoor pixies. My excitement was tempered by disappointment that no other member of my family was anywhere near me to witness the event. My cousin, who had set out with me for an afternoon walk across the moor to a nearby tor, had sometime back chosen a different route, so by now we were quite a long way apart. I shouted across to where I could see her, to draw her attention to the phenomenon on the skyline, but she did not hear me.

It may have been my shout that did it. I shall never know. For one minute they were there. The next they had gone. I ran as fast as I could up the side of the hill to where I had last seen them, but alas, when I reached the top, and could look across the open moor, there was no sign of anyone. They had vanished into thin air. I hunted everywhere; I so much wished to meet and talk with them. But it was not to be. So, disconsolately, I trudged on to rejoin my cousin and tell her all about my astonishing experience.

She of course refused to believe a word I said, which annoyed me greatly.

Mind you, all this happened a long time ago when I was a child, only eleven or so, and my imagination was a lot livelier and fresher than it is now. But was it any less accurate because of that?

I have never met anyone else who claims to have seen the pixies, in cold blood as it were, and adult reason dully suggests that what I saw was either an optical illusion (perhaps some sort of mirage) or, of course, some real people, perhaps a family of small children dressed up. But if so, how did they manage to disappear among the tussocks of heather?

I continue to prefer my original interpretation.

Cieran Madden

ACTRESS

New Hall etc.
Feb. 10th

Darling Mummy & Daddy,

Thank you so much for the letters. I'm writing to Auntie Marge today. I have size 34 in Brassières. Please could you send my locket and chain by next weekend. I quite see the Head's point of view in the quest of science, but instead of going to the two weekly sessions of it I have ballet and music instead.

The new mistress is very nice and a good teacher but *not* a good pianist. She said I had excellent fingerwork, my scales in the tune were very fast and even & I was very musical and I felt 'Purr Purr!' She's a *very* good teacher.

I have been very good indeed in class and I've been copying notes and things and really trying & the result was that I got *much* better marks in Latin & I think French (because I know I've done a good Ex. this weekend). But I've been naughty in our room *so* many times i.e. laughing and talking, that I'm not sure but I might have to go into a dormitory. But if not, I'm going to be really good!! – of course even if I am changed I'll be good. I haven't been showing off.

I'm enclosing a letter from *Fer* to me, it arrived as I got back on Saturday which was awfully nice. So I wrote to him on Sunday & John & Alexandra.

I'm going to see what the number of my first term's Christmas Play when I was an angel's photographs are and write them *done* in this letter together with the name of the photographer and you can write to him & ask for the negatives. The two Ref. Nos. to the 2 photos were Ref. No. 7175/C, Ref. No. 7175/I, address given at end of letter.

I love you!! Yes, I will get the records when I come out.

Please darling Mummy and Daddy, could you buy these things and if they're too expensive I'll pay for half, just take it out of my savings. It's for a dance our house is giving the school. here there are: = cheeze, crisps, sardines, cocoa, mustard. If it's altogether *too* much could you send one or two of the items – but we would love them all!!!!!!!!!!!!

Our house is completely different now, it only consists of our class which is 16 children – before it was about 34 with most of class IV in but they've moved up so we've got all the big home, comfy chairs and sofas to ourselves. It's much nicer!!

For our dance we've all *got* to wear masks, but not like the dance. *Fer* & I went to buy bird's masks and animals masks. I've got nothing to make mine with here do you think you could send me something or concoct something from my other mask which I carefully put away in my chest of drawers (the ones belonging to my dressing-table on the top left-hand drawer). *Please!* because I could make something with the remaining piece of mask material and buckrum & please if I'm very careful could I have a few pretty stones and things to stick on with that marvellous glue. Oh dear! I'm asking you to send me an *awful* lot.

But please + this is the parcel = Mask, material, pritts, buckrum, good for dance, brassière 34″, locket & chain. *Please!!* could you send them. The whole school will be eternally grateful! Please give my love to Charles-Wharles. I love you.

Please write to me & send the parcel – but I forgot please send the food *only* by the 1st of *March* sharp will you, because it will be stale long before the party begins but if you could send the other things by next weekend it would be lovely! This is the photographer's address

Ron. Francis, London Road

lots of love, hugs, kisses & sandadies love from Ci xoxo

Nigel Mansell

RACING DRIVER

I learned to drive on a farm at Whythall. It was owned by the parents of one of my Wellsbourne school-mates, Michael Webster, whom I haven't seen or spoken to for years. We were about ten and used to drive a battered old Austin Seven around the farm land. We had some fantastic adventures, driving this thing through fields with such long grass you couldn't see further than the bonnet. I suppose we were doing only about 10 or 15 mph, but it was exhilarating, all right. We had a few spills, of course, but it was just good fun. I didn't think at that time that I had any particular driving skills. It was just something we did.

Christopher Martin-Jenkins

I suppose most boys who become infatuated with cricket at an early age dream of playing for their country, and no doubt most of them play imaginary Test matches. Not only was I no exception, but I actually spent the whole of my spare time playing garden cricket, except during blizzards and severe thunderstorms (but they had to *be* severe) when the game would be transferred to my bedroom and continued with a toy rifle as the bat and a ping-pong ball, which swung and spun devilishly.

I appreciate that even this all-consuming passion was probably far from unique, but what was different, I believe, about my games was the men who played them. You see, I genuinely had to imagine myself a real member of the England team and whereas others might see themselves playing alongside Hutton or Compton or Graveney or May, I found this too unrealistic. So instead I willed myself forward in time and invented the England team of the future, of which I was the charming modest, talented and much admired captain.

In the great England side of this imagined era (I suppose logically, if I was to play a part, it should have been the 1970s, but in fact when I put a date at the top of a scorecard it was usually somewhere in the 2050s – a hundred years on). In this side I was both opening batsman and opening bowler. I rarely failed to make a big score, and I played all the strokes although, for the sake of realism, I was not impregnable. The running commentary (by myself) which always accompanied the whole match, spoke of grace, power and enterprise. My driving had rarely been equalled in the history of the game. Peter May perhaps had been equally good on the on side; Len Hutton, Tom Graveney and Colin Cowdrey on the off; but few if any had achieved such an all-round mastery. If I did fail – and one played against some formidable overseas bowling – I usually made up for it with a devastating spell of outswing bowling. Some of the figures I achieved in Test matches were the equal of anything Spofforth, Barnes, Trueman or Lindwall ever produced.

But this was no one-man team. My opening partner was my brother, a plucky red-haired left hander. I used to think that he did not quite have the same natural ability, the same extraordinary power and range of stroke, but what a competitor, and what a prolific run getter! He *had* to be, for when I was not playing Tests by myself, he was playing them with me, and the game had to be interesting for both.

Number three: now that was a problem position. How many hours did the fraternal selectors spend, late at night, discussing who would do this important job best. No one ever quite established himself, but more often than not Robin Smaels, son of a man who had been Nottinghamshire captain at the turn of the twenty-first century, was chosen. Looking uncannily like M.J.K. Smith, he was a bad starter, but, if he got going a tall, elegant stroke player and also a very fine close fielder. Some newspapers annoyingly persisted in spelling his name Smales: it was not, it was Smaels.

Paul Gruché made number four his own. Here was a man with all the shots, another Denis Compton in his lifestyle and his batting style. About five foot ten, with strong wrists and shoulders, dark, casual, handsome – the son of a French actor, oddly enough. He played, by the way, for Middlesex, and I suppose, though quite unconsciously, he was modelled a bit on Compton.

At number five, Russell Prince. The name explained the man: regal, dashing, young, haughty. Although he played for several years, he remained the young promising member of the team, permanently in his third year at Cambridge, gloriously continuing the amateur tradition.

At six and seven came two more all-rounders: Calthorpe, a very swift opening bowler off a short run and a batsman who had genuine class; and Bob Crale, captain of Gloucestershire, a loyal man, red-faced, from a farming family; a lusty hitter and a steady medium-paced bowler who could swing it both ways. A man who often came good in a crisis.

The spinners were not always the same. David Angus, Marlborough and Oxford educated, was usually the off-spinner, though he had not yet fully mastered the accuracy and the power of spin which had made his predecessor, Bill Brazier of Surrey, the best of his type since Laker a hundred years before. Brazier himself occasionally made an emotional comeback in my games.

Angus, by the way, played for Warwickshire. He rarely, if ever, went through a Test series with the same spinning partner (indeed he more than once lost his own place to Dicky Grenville, another off-spinner with a slinging action who spun the ball devastatingly but lacked control). The left arm rivals were Pullin of Gloucestershire and E.W.W. Macer of Derbyshire. Pullin, with an action extraordinarily reminiscent of Johnny Wardle, usually got my vote. If a leg spinner was selected it was usually Billy Kent, an eccentric young Surrey player who was also a pop singer.

There was never any doubt about who should take the new ball. It had to be Mike Brackley, a Yorkshireman through and through; dark, rugged, outspoken, from mining stock of course. He used to be a bit of an embarrassment to me on tour sometimes, but Mike and I got on well and he was a ferocious bowler to have on your side.

As for the wicket-keeper, although in the twentieth century Kent might have enjoyed something of a monopoly, Lancashire took over in the twenty-first, because the three who held the spot during and just after my playing days were all Lancastrians: 'jumping' Johnny Vasser, his young brother Bob, and later, perhaps the most immaculate of them all, Ken Potter. Jumping Johnny Vasser got his name one summer holiday in North Wales, which my brother and I spent diving around in the sand dunes, taking brilliant catches with a hard little rubber ball from Woolworths.

These men lived for me, blissfully happy people who, even amidst the dreariness of a Latin or Maths period, could be called instantly to mind to relieve the boredom.

As for the garden cricket, as soon as I had a lawn just about big enough for a Test match again I began working on my own children in the hope that they would get the same innocent enjoyment from it that I had done. I just give them the odd subtle hint, such as buying them bats, balls and stumps, mowing out a pitch, and offering to play with them. They are both keen cricketers now, but, alas, they have never played a garden Test match in their lives. Perhaps my boyhood imaginings were not, after all, so commonplace.

Hayley Mills

ACTRESS

Ode to Hamlet

'Death's Black Wings'
So famous was Shakespear's Hamlet
Known the whole world o'er
But no-one knows of my Hamlet
Who's death caused no horrified awe,
Only to me, my friend and confider.
Buried in solitude – blissfully sleeping
Hammy – Oh! Hammy, why did you leave me?
Buried you are 'neath the old poplar tree,
Unknowing, uncaring, how your death affected me.

I wish death was like roses
When life's long race is won
Leaves only it's petals,
And soon there are none.
To be blown by the wind
On a soft summer breeze
Away and away like the red autumn leaves
Silent, untroublesome, elusive as night to lie on the
        wind in a heavenly flight.

Age 14

Sir John Mills CBE

ACTOR

The first clear pictures that emerge from the montage of my early childhood days come from Belton, a small village near Great Yarmouth in Norfolk where my father held the post of headmaster at the local school. We lived in the small school house where conditions were primitive. The water supply came from a pump in the yard which also housed the 'thunder box', as my father termed the loo, a small wooden building containing a large wooden seat in which were three holes of different sizes – large, medium and small. One morning, deciding that I must establish at least to myself that I was growing up fast, I chose to perch myself over the hole reserved for my father. All went well until I reached for the sports page of the *Daily Mail*, cut into quarters and hung by a string from a nail in the wall. My reach was too short; I lost my balance and descended into the abyss. My screams brought Aunty Betty, all of four feet three inches, who took one look at my head below the surface and promptly fainted. Somewhat later, smelling strongly of Wright's Coal Tar soap, I was required by my father to copy out three times:

> I must always pause
> Before I sit
> And choose a size that
> Is meant to fit
> A very small boy

I considered this to be unjust, and also the rhyme seemed to lack bite, so I inserted an 'h' into the last word of the second line. Shortly afterwards I discovered that a ruler could be put to other uses besides measuring.

David Money-Coutts

CHAIRMAN OF COUTTS AND COMPANY

When I was about twelve I was allowed on one occasion to have dinner in the dining room, rather than on a tray in my bedroom, when staying with my grandparents. At that age one is concerned to do the right thing and I knew, of course, that soup should be slurped from the side of the spoon rather than poured quietly into one's mouth from the end.

What I was not prepared for was having the soup served in little lidded pots standing in the soup plates rather than ladled into the plates. Mistake number one was to pour the soup out of the pot (*away* from me) into the plate; apparently it should be poured *towards* oneself in order to see what is happening and so that, if any is spilled, it will not take the polish off the table but merely take the skin off the pourer. This lesson was learned with no great embarrassment, the empty pot placed on my side plate – never put a hot dish on the table – and I settled down to slurping the soup into my hungry mouth.

Suddenly, on my left hand, there was the butler proffering a tray with more lidded soup pots. Now the soup was delicious but I thought that a well brought-up young man should not have a second helping of the first course. 'No, thank you,' I said. The po-faced Adams remained firmly by my side. Collapse of small boy in great embarrassment when it was pointed out that the pots on the butler's tray were the *empties* he was collecting.

Patrick Moore OBE

AMATEUR ASTRONOMER

I have one memory of childhood – it goes back to the age of eleven, and it is vivid even now (it goes back to the year 1934). This was about the only term I managed at prep school; from the age of seven to fifteen I was ill most of the time (at sixteen I swindled my age and medical and got into the RAF as air crew, but that's another story). Anyway, at eleven there I was. Never had I been able to play any games; I hadn't been fit enough. But after a couple of weeks all seemed well, and I was put into the Second Game at cricket – the first time in my life.

My side batted first. I went in last. The first ball was enough for me; out. Clean bowled. Never mind; they had to bat next. I was put into the field (I had no idea where to go) and dropped a catch at once. Then, for some obscure reason, the master in charge asked if I could bowl. I had to admit that I'd never tried. 'Well,' he said, 'take the ball – hold it like this – and see if you can.'

With trepidation I took the ball. How far should I run back? Six or seven paces? I decided on ten. There was the batsman; and *I was actually going to play cricket* like all other boys. It seemed unbelievable.

I ran up, and bowled. I know I put spin on it; I afterwards found that it was a leg-break – the first I'd ever seen, so far as I know – and it hit the batsman's middle stump. So with my first ball I took a wicket, and I will never forget the thrill of it.

In fact I took three more wickets that afternoon. It was my only game; next week I was laid low again, and I didn't pick up a bat or a cricket ball again until I was sixteen. I suppose that's why, at the age of sixty-five (and therefore qualifying as a Senior Citizen or, in my own terms, an Old Coot) I still play regularly, and hope to get my hundred wickets per season. I have lost count of the number of leg-breaks I have bowled in my time. But all the same, I'll never forget the first one of all!

Cliff Morgan CVO, OBE

BROADCASTER AND RUGBY INTERNATIONAL

On my mother's knee, I learned, not nursery rhymes, but the fact that the New Zealand rugby player, Bob Deans, did not score against Wales at Cardiff Arms Park in 1905. Perhaps it was not the very first thing I recall, for in our house, my mother taught me from birth The Lord's Prayer and the National Anthem.

There was never a moment without music. From across the street came the sound of hymn tunes being sung in the chapel. That sound has remained in my subconscious. Although I learned the piano and viola and eventually came to appreciate the beauty of Mozart, Brahms and Chopin, it's the hymn tunes that really touch me for they are fine tunes.

Little did I know then that when I eventually played rugby for Wales that 'Cwm Rhondda' and others would be sung by the crowds in perfect harmony and prove to be worth at least a dozen points to Wales. The sounds that dominated my life as a baby for some reason inspired a superhuman effort on the field of play.

My father carried me on his back to and from choir practice twice a week . . . up and down a hill which had an incline of one in nine. Before I was ten I knew the soprano, alto, tenor and bass parts of the *Messiah, Elijah, Twelfth Mass* and *Creation* – and do you know that when I eventually sang in the choir with my mother and father, I had as much laughter and delight as touring the world with rugby teams.

I was walking out of the clubhouse at Cardiff Arms Park at midnight, the day, as the Welsh insist, when we were narrowly beaten 24 points to 6 by Scotland! A friend of mine took the keys of his car from his pocket and threw them to his pal. 'Evan, you'll have to drive. You're too drunk to sing!!'

What would my mother have said?

John Motson
TELEVISION SPORTS COMMENTATOR

I grew up in south London but most of my childhood holidays were spent in Lincolnshire, because my parents both came from Boston families. In those days, a day at the seaside meant Skegness, where I once fell in a paddling pool and hated the water for the rest of my life, or Sutton-on-Sea, where a donkey ride along the beach was the highlight of the day.

All my relatives, uncles, aunties, grandparents and cousins, lived in Lincolnshire, and although I have since travelled all over the world I still regard it as my spiritual home in many ways. My father was a Methodist minister, my grandfather and uncle were local preachers, so the village chapel in the Fens was another childhood memory.

I suppose the thing I miss about it most is the old railway line. In those days the train from King's Cross to Boston would stop at all the village stations between Peterborough and Spalding, and between Spalding and Boston. Now most of them are obsolete and part of the lines has been ripped up.

Modern life has become streamlined and far more convenient, but the old order had its distinctive standards and more's the pity some of them don't still apply.

Countess Mountbatten of Burma
CD, JP, DL

Air-raid Warning

Evacuated to New York during the Second World War, I wrote this piece for my school magazine when aged sixteen.

Those first few air-raid warnings at school early this summer were mere pleasure outings compared with what they must be now; but still, to us who had never experienced anything more than a practice one before, they certainly were exciting.

The school had moved from London to a large country house in the south of England when the war came. Apart from such things as identification cards and ration-books, which didn't seriously hinder one's appetite, the war didn't affect us much. True we helped get in the hay and laboriously collected wood and fir cones, spurred on by the remembrances of last winter's bitter cold and few fires, and the thoughts of the coming winter which would undoubtedly be worse. Knitting warm blankets and garments for the fighting men took up most of our spare time. We had been taught in what position to fling ourselves to the ground should a dive-bomber feel inclined to use us as practice targets, which of course would be great fun for the bomber, but would not exactly be our idea of entertainment. Rehearsals for air-raid warnings were also frequently held but lacked the spice of the real thing.

The first real air-raid warnings started in air bases along the north coast of France. As we were not far from the Channel, the reconnaissance planes and bombers passed directly over the school. As soon as the planes were sighted over the coast, about thirty miles away, the warning was sent through: 'Yellow light.' This meant that the enemy planes were still a fair distance away, and we were allowed to sleep on in peace. If, however, the warning, 'Red Light' came through, this meant that the planes were in the near vicinity and we were hauled out of bed in double-quick time. The air-raid warnings always came at about 1:00 a.m. and lasted with extraordinarily regularity till about 4:30 a.m. By timing it this way the Germans could reach their objectives and return to their home bases before dawn came, and the protecting darkness disappeared. Very often we

Left: Peter de Savary, aged three
Above: Sir Archibald Ross, aged three
Below: The Rev. the Lord Soper (middle, front row in Eton collar and bow) at school in 1913 in Wandsworth, west London

Left: A self-portrait by Norman Thelwell, drawn aged ten

Below: Shaw Taylor (left) with his family on the beach at Ramsgate

could hear the drone of the engines as the planes passed overhead, and see the long white tentacles of the searchlight beams criss-crossing the quiet night sky in numbers as they tried to locate their prey. Later on we began to distinguish between the steady purr of the British engines and the irregular beat of the Germans if we happened to be awake when they came over.

As soon as the warning came through, the mistresses would go to all the girls' rooms and rouse the sleepy inmates none too gently. We soon got so used to this that before we were properly awake we would already be out of bed and slipping on thick coats and socks. Blankets and gas-masks we took down to the cellars every evening before going to bed to save time in case they should be wanted. Having snatched up pillows we groped our way downstairs holding on to the person in front with one hand; the impenetrable darkness filled with the rustle of clothes and the pad-padding of many slippered feet on carpet and board; the stifling blackness penetrated only by hushed voices and reassuring laughs. We weren't frightened, but there was an excited tense atmosphere which sent tingles up one's spine, and the threatening drone of powerful engines in the dark sky above told us this was the real thing.

Arrived at the rather murky, airless safety of the cellar we all had a lot of fun sitting wrapped in our blankets, singing at the top of our voices, or telling stories, munching chocolate and biscuits. In fact we all quite looked forward to the frequent warnings, especially the eight- and nine-year olds who regarded it as the greatest treat being awakened and allowed to play in the middle of the night.

The cellar was luckily of the enormous, rambling kind found in old country houses and easily accommodated the sixty-odd girls and staff, although towards the end of the time the air became unpleasantly stuffy. An enormous barrel, reaching almost to the ceiling, stood in the middle of the floor; legend has it that King Charles I hid in it while fleeing from Cromwell's troops in the seventeenth century. He must have felt somewhat as we did hiding there three centuries later. Boards on trestles were set around the cellar and covered with newspapers, mats, pieces of carpet, anything that came in handy and was fairly soft to lie on; also cotton mattress covers were filled with straw and these made quite comfortable mattresses except that they rustled abominably at the slightest movement. We slept in rows, about two to one mattress. This had one advantage of enabling one to keep warm. Trying to sleep was not made any easier by the deafening snores of some people and the noisy whimpering of the two dogs which belonged to one of the girls and were doubtless dreaming of rabbits. Occasionally the distant drone of planes could be heard and we wondered what was happening to parents and families in other parts of the country.

Sleeping under these conditions was none too easy, but like anything else it could be done, and gradually as we got used to it, it became a habit. Another habit which soon developed was that of subconsciously jumping out of bed and beginning to put on coat and slippers if ever one was awakened during the night. This can become quite a tiresome habit when it isn't at all necessary.

The 'All Clear' usually came through at about 4:30 a.m. and we thankfully gathered up our belongings. Sleepily we trouped upstairs to bed for the remaining few hours of the night in the grey light of the first few streaks of dawn in the paling sky.

Frank Muir CBE
WRITER AND BROADCASTER

It was the perfect holiday. I remember packing my suitcase with tremendous care, emptying it out and beginning again until everything lay in neat and unruffled order. I was travelling alone so I planned the journey carefully and rehearsed it endlessly in my mind. When the day came, I bade farewell to my loved ones and set off. I had four days of bliss and returned home, safely, with my memories. I was aged six, and I had gone to my grandmother's house, four doors down the road.

No holiday since has quite lived up to that one.

As a matter of fact, I did not go away on holiday again until I was grown-up. As I lived at the seaside there was nowhere better to go away *to*. I was once taken into the countryside for a day and I was appalled. We lived at Broadstairs and I sang in the choir at the parish church. Or, to be more accurate, I turned up but did not actually give voice. The lure of the choir was the five shillings a quarter that the job paid. My only hope of hanging on to this bonanza was to conceal from the authorities the fact that I could not sing (a fact only too clear to Radio 4 listeners) and so I developed a technique of lurking in the background at all times and, during hymns, miming.

Another bonus to being a songster was the Annual Choir Outing. The vicar laid on a horsebrake. This was an ancient Edwardian vehicle which had plied between Ramsgate and Pegwell Bay until it became so unroadworthy that no horse could be persuaded to pull it. We all sat on plank seats facing each other, I and two other voiceless delinquents on the uncovered top deck, and proceeded in a light, warm, summer drizzle towards the Kent village of Pluck's Gutter (what magic names these old hamlets have, to be sure).

We arrived at our picnic spot very late as the horse turned petulant just north of Sandwich and slowed to 1mph but the vicar soon had us deployed in a circle on the meadow grass, clutching our brawn sandwiches. 'We are now,' he announced with a ring in his voice, 'in the midst of Nature!'

In which case, was the choristers' unspoken thought, the sooner this holiday is over and we get back to smelly seaweed and damp sand, the better.

If your bottom is uncomfortable on sand you merely have to wiggle a bit and the sand conforms to your shape. Nature does not do this. You sit on a tussock and what happens? A sharp piece of long grass goes up the leg of your shorts causing brief agony, you are tilted sideways causing you to drop your brawn sandwich into a small but active community of black beetles, and the suspiciously warm patch on which you are now sitting is a reminder that this is pasture on which sheep have safely grazed.

Nature, of which there is a considerable quantity in the countryside, is full of fauna, as well as prickly flora which scratches your ankles. The seaside has little bits of fauna but these are mostly harmless and frequently edible, e.g., shrimps. Insect life at the seaside is benign, mostly a few little hopping things in the sand. Nature, on the other hand, offers whole regiments of malevolent predators whose tiny little teeth do damage far in excess of the beast's height and fighting weight. For anybody collecting this kind of scientific data, I am able to state that during forty minutes spent in a meadow adjacent to Pluck's Gutter, Kent, sitting half on a tussock and half on firmish sheep spoor, the following happened: a very large shiny, black bug, clearly in wine, flew erratically in front of me and then thudded into my forehead. A weal arose. A colony of frantic, maladjusted, and very tiny ants invaded my sandals and scurried about, biting. About two hundred thousand very small red marks arose. A cricket levitated in front of me and dropped down the front of my shirt causing me to utter a long, thin, girlish scream. A squadron of large flies with hairy legs and, by the sound of them, jet engines, strafed me and my brawn. A number of ugly lumps arose on forehead and forearms. I threw the brawn away.

How much more preferable was that holiday, years earlier, with my grandmother.

Dame Iris Murdoch DBE

Earliest Childhood Memory

I am sitting up in my pram crowing with delight. The pram is running down a slight incline. My mother, who has let go of the pram, is running after it, laughing, very beautiful.

Derek Nimmo

ACTOR, WRITER AND PRODUCER

The best bit of advice heavily instilled into me at an early age by my dear mother was a little couplet that goes as follows:

> Good, better, best
> Never let it rest
> Until the good is better
> And the better, best.

It is something I have always remembered and have constantly although rarely successfully tried to achieve.

John Julius Norwich

AUTHOR AND BROADCASTER

One of the clearest of my early memories is of when, at the age of six, I was taken abroad by my mother for the first time. As we walked along the platform of the Gare de Lyon looking for our *wagon-lit* I distinctly remember a large, fat, florid and furious Englishman in a deafening altercation with a cowering railway official. I can hear his words now, pronounced with a Churchill-ian English accent: 'Non, non, non – je pay Cooks, Cooks pay voo!'

Claire Oberman

ACTRESS

When I was five or six years old we were living out in the backblocks on a farm, and as at that stage I was still an only child, I was very pleased to have my little friend from school (who lived in town) to stay the night. My parents were milking cows in the cowshed which was down a driveway past some fields, a good way away from the house. There were gardens, the orchard, the barn, and outbuildings in between. My friend (her father was the doctor who brought me into the world!) Gillian Lamb and I were having our bath, at five o'clock or so and we had finishing playing and making the taps all sorts of exotic machinery and playing offices with the soap dish as typewriter and so on and were lying back, one at each end of the bath telling each other stories turn about. The tales changed from re-runs of 'Hansel and Gretel' to more improvised sagas of woe and horror. As we tried to outdo each other in inventive-ness (our imaginations working overtime) the stories got worse and worse! From wolves we graduated to elves, witches, evil giants and horror to end all horrors – ghosts!! As we fell silent in breathless awe at our vivid creations, every creak and rustle in the silent empty house magnified out of all proportion and intensified our fear as we looked into each other's black and round terror-filled eyes, convinced we were about to be haunted to death. In unison we sprang out of the bath and ran screaming down the track, our feet not feeling the stones, past the orchard and the buildings to the cowshed for the fortitude it held.

My parents to this day say that the milk production was down that night because two little naked banshees curdled the milk in their udders!

Charles Osborne

AUTHOR

An Antipodean Childhood

Brisbane in the 1920s and 1930s had the aspect of an overgrown country town. Its population was around 300,000, its sub-tropical climate brought pleasant, mild winters which were all too short, and long, sweltering summers whose relentless sunshine was punctuated by thunderstorms which people always said would 'bring a little relief' but which never did. Or perhaps I did not recognize the kind of relief they brought. In the north of the state lay the tropical part of Queensland, the rain forests, the coral reefs, the crocodile-infested rivers, the aborigine settlements. We never dreamed of going up there. 'It isn't white man's country,' my father used to say. I found it easy to believe him for I didn't think that even Brisbane was white man's country.

The suburb in which we lived consisted of several hills, a regular little Rome though with a different kind of architecture. The wooden houses were built on stilts. We lived in one of the bigger houses, but when I was twelve we moved a few hundred yards to a smaller one. The streets were wide, unpaved and dusty, and the only shade-giving trees were in people's back yards.

My parents, who seemed to me while they lived to be amiable but ordinary, I now perceive to have been (my mother especially) rather extraordinary.

I spent my first twelve years in a house on top of a hill, with large grounds. The earth was stony. I remember no grass, only a grape vine and some ferns. I could feel the curve of the land as I pedalled across it in my red toy motor-car, and I believed that what I could feel was the earth's curvature – one of those absent-minded lies my father told me. I remember, too, my father's kisses, which tasted of what I identified years later as claret. There were roses in the front garden, but the roses I remember most clearly are those which formed the pattern on the linoleum in the kitchen. As a two-year-old I would sniff at them, intrigued by their lack of perfume. When I was four I already experienced a kind of nostalgia for the innocence of childhood, for I knew by then the difference between reality and its representation.

Shortly after my fourth birthday I began to attend the kindergarten in our suburb of Paddington. My mother took me every morning and came to bring me home again at midday. What on earth did we *Kinder* do there? Sang terrible songs, I suppose, and, oh yes, were made to eat apples. I was continually hiding apples with one reluctant bite taken out of them. To this day the apple is a fruit I do not willingly eat.

Peter O'Sullevan OBE
RACING COMMENTATOR

I was seven at the time. I know that because it was the year, 1925, that Double Chance won the Grand National. Although born in Ireland, I was brought up in England by my grandparents as my Irish father and English mother had separated. My grandmother was a keen horsewoman and the weekend guests, who would be going out with the Old Surrey & Burstow, had brought four horses with them. I remember being very upset and I went missing. The staff were questioned, apparently, including the Russian chef who was my friend, and who would have been quite capable of hiding me so that I could avoid the horror of tea, and polite conversation, in the drawing-room. But he hadn't. My bicycle was in its proper place. Neither Truelove, the head groom, or Pattenden, the chauffeur, who lived in a cottage at the end of the drive (labour was cheap in that era, but power was exercised with responsibility) had set eyes on 'Master Peter'. My grandfather called the constabulary.

It was raining and the guests' horses had necessitated some rearrangement in the stable yard. The police telephoned late in the afternoon to inform Sir John Henry that a small boy had been spotted from the Merstham–Reigate road in the middle of a large paddock, holding an umbrella over a chestnut pony. The protest worked. Fairy, a name ill-suited to the macho pony he was, was reaccommodated inside.

As a patron of the International League for the Protection of Horses and the Brooke Hospital for Animals, Cairo, I have been trying to hold up the umbrella ever since.

Childhood Memories

The Rt. Hon. Dr David Owen MP
LEADER OF THE SDP

One day in the autumn of 1945 I was summoned by the headmaster, who told me to go to the front porch as my mother and sister had come to take me out. With them was a strange man with a moustache. I went up to them, shook hands with the stranger who asked me my name. 'Owen, sir,' I said. 'In that case I'm your father,' he said. He had just been demobilized from the war. Our relationship then got off to a bad start. We went to lunch at a local pub. This was a time when rations were still very short. To my delight, I saw that spotted dick pudding was on the menu. Raisins were a luxury. When it arrived, I picked out all the raisins and carefully put them on the side of my plate to have as a marvellous treat at the end of my meal. I had just finished the pudding, and was gazing at my raisins like the fat boy in *Pickwick Papers*, when suddenly my father leaned forward, put out an enormous, it seemed to me, hand, scooped them up and ate them. It was years before I believed that my father, seeing me extract the raisins and put them on the edge of my plate, concluded I didn't like raisins, and that since he did, *he* would have them.

Peter Palumbo
ARCHITECT AND CHAIRMAN OF THE ARTS COUNCIL

At the tender age of six I was bundled off to boarding-school in the country by my parents to escape London and the threat of Hitler's bombs. End-of-term reports had already become a well-established ritual and they always followed the same pattern: the summons to my father's study, with its desk, photographs and pipe-rack; its fireplace, breakfront bookcase and piles of periodicals and journals stacked on the floor around the margins of the room. My father would clean, fill and light his pipe in a deliberate sort of way, while I stood at the far side of the desk. I remember feeling slightly irritated at the cat, which had made its home on the chair that I would have sat on, had I been invited to do so. My father read aloud the standard remarks of the various masters, looking in vain for a hint of distinction in his only son. 'Lethargic indifference, but brightens at the sight of food.' 'Good God!' my father exclaimed, his eyes twinkling. 'The man's a genius. He has got you in one.'

As usual he was right.

Derek Parker

AUTHOR AND BROADCASTER

All Miss Mildren's Fault

I had assumed that teachers were put into the world to make one miserable. I had fallen deeply in love with my first, at the age of five or six, and she deserted me, going off in a flood of tears (mine, not her's) to employment elsewhere; then came Miss May, whose chief delight was walking along the rows of desks and assaulting one from behind, when least expected and for the most minor of reasons ('Sit up straight – *CLUMP*'). There were one or two others, too; they may have loved dogs, but they certainly weren't very keen on children.

However, in 1942 or thereabouts, came Miss Mildren. She must have been, I suppose, in her twenties, and she clearly believed in the pleasure principle, and what she taught me about was books – or, rather, reading. This didn't happen, in my house. Well, it happened to the extent of the *Daily Express*, which in those days was a respectable newspaper; and to the extent of the *News of the World* – not quite as respectable, and bits of it slightly puzzling to the average reader of the *Dandy* or *Beano*.

The *Dandy* and *Beano* were books. My mother's weekly book was *Woman's Own*. Don't misunderstand me: my parents knew all about the importance of being able to read. I could read before I went to school – I can shut my eyes and see my first reading book, now; Sunday mornings in bed, Mum on one side, Dad on the other, and my diminutive self, knowing at the age of four just when to turn over. But knowing how to read and knowing about reading aren't the same things.

School wasn't a lot of help. There, books existed, but were meant as instruments of torture – full of entirely uninteresting statements about something called geography or arithmetic or even English, but no pictures or conversations, and chiefly valuable, it seemed as an excuse for inflicting corporal punishment ('Don't know what a predicative adjective is?' – *WHAM!*).

But, then came Miss Mildren, hand in paw with Winnie-the-Pooh. I can remember with total clarity the rainy afternoon when she read us the story of the Horrible Heffalump. I can't think what she was up to: I'm quite sure it wasn't a part of the curriculum. But anyway, for whatever reason, she read it, and read it marvellously. It was the first time I had been actually helpless with laughter – falling-down drunk with it.

On the way home, I thoughtfully realized that all that laughter, all that fun, had come out of a book. A book with hard covers on it. Out of the activity of reading.

I got *The House at Pooh Corner* out of my Auntie Phyllis next Christmas (very eccentric, that request was considered). And discovered, of course, that there was more than laughter: I still can't read the last page of it without crying.

Julia Parker

ASTROLOGER

Looking for the Meaning

It all began in bed.

In bed on Sunday morning, when, as usual, aged seven, I'd made morning tea and taken it up to my parents in bed, with oval Marie biscuits and the Sunday newspapers.

'Read the stars – read the stars!' one of us would cry, and either Mummy, Daddy or I – whoever had finished the umpteenth oval Marie or cup of tea, would oblige . . .

'Let's see – Gemini . . . Oh, that's good – you're going to have a nice week. Wednesday looks promising!' Mummy would say: 'And now, Libra . . .'

'But what about Leo?' I'd butt in (and sure as eggs, Leos were going to be extravagant).

'Now don't you spend all your wages at once!' (Pocket money was always 'wages' in our house, and I used to get a raise of a penny a week each time I passed a music or dancing exam.)

Pause. More tea, more oval Maries.

'But Mummy – what is Gemini, what *is* Leo . . .?'

Another pause. For thought, this time.

'Well, dear,' (Mummy's typically drawling Libran voice would eventually reply) '*I'm* Libra, *Daddy's* Gemini, and *you're* Leo.'

'Oh, Mummy, I know – but what does it *mean?*'

A longer pause.

'Well dear – *Daddy's* Gemini, *I'm* Libra . . .'

They never told me what it meant. Maybe if they had, I'd never have become an astrologer! But then, Mummy still has a drawing I did at that time, of comets, planets and the Moon, all hanging above beautiful castles and palaces. Typical Leo, that's me.

Nicholas Parsons

RADIO AND TELEVISION PRESENTER

One of the most vivid and exciting experiences in a young child's life is when he or she sees a live show for the first time. To a young and impressionable mind there is something magical about the atmosphere of a live show in a large theatre, with real people performing, as opposed to the visual images they see on their television screens. This not only fires their imagination, but for many leaves a lasting impression that stays for the whole of their lives. I have had the joy and privilege of seeing this at first hand, when working in pantomime, and looking over the footlights into the rapt, eager and expectant faces as they gaze with wonder and amazement at all that is taking place on the stage. My first experience of live entertainment was the circus, and I have never forgotten it. It happened in Grantham, the small Lincolnshire market town where I was born, and spent the early years of my life. My father was a family doctor, and we lived in a large house overlooking the green in the centre of the town. In those prewar days there was no television, and even little radio, so an entertainment visiting the town was a huge excitement. I remember seeing from our nursery window the circus lorries and trailers arriving as they moved to a site where the Big Top was to be erected, and was fascinated by the elephants plodding along in file, each holding the tail of the one in front with his trunk. Later an open lorry with clowns and jugglers on board slowly toured the town, drumming up interest and promoting the circus as well as handing out leaflets.

Eventually the day arrived when my older brother, younger sister and I were taken by my parents to the show, which was probably quite a modest touring circus, but the memory of everything that went to make up that entertainment is indelibly imprinted on my mind.

I remember the ringmaster in his red coat, and though I had no wish to emulate him in his authoritative job, it is interesting that in my later years I have become a chairman of panel games, a compere and a host of a quiz show. I was fascinated by the animals, awestruck by the trapeze artists, loved the clowns and was thrilled by the acrobats – particularly the act where two of them jumped on and off a horse that slowly cantered round the ring, and they did tricks while balancing on the broad back of the horse.

The memory of that visit to the circus in Grantham is still with me, and if proof were needed that my destiny was to be in the entertainment profession – though I did become an engineer first to please my family – the first thing I did when we returned home was to start taking off the clowns and trying to emulate the tumblers. Later, with the help of my brother, John, we put together our own circus entertainment in the nursery, and invited our parents and other relations to see it. John was the ringmaster, my sister, Patricia, who was only three, and I appeared as the show horses, scampering around on our hands and knees in response to the orders of my brother. I then did a tumbling act on a mattress, and our little sister was then instructed to be a trapeze artist, which in a flood of tears she quite rightly said was not possible. We compromised and let her go on as a solo horse, which she loved, while John and I changed and then came out as the two clowns we had seen in the circus, who called themselves 'Cuckoo' and 'Sparrow'. We tried to reproduce their routine, which mostly consisted of me using a catch phrase, which Cuckoo – the put-upon one or straighter of the two clowns – used to his partner whenever he was lost or confused. He simply appealed to Sparrow in a cooing voice, saying 'Cuckoo . . . Sparrow'. For weeks the house echoed to the sound of me going around calling out, 'Cuckoo . . . Sparrow', until my parents, growing bored with the repetition, told me to stop being such a clown and keep my antics for the nursery.

Those two clowns, probably now long dead, could never have realized as they performed their simple routine one afternoon in the town of Grantham, the effect they had on an impressionable five-year-old, and awoke in him a passion for show business that has never waned, and given him a childhood memory that will stay all his life.

Sir John Paul GCMG, OBE, MC
FORMER GOVERNOR-GENERAL TO CROWN DEPENDENCIES

My brother and I were very proud of our big black cars. They were pedal-driven of course but we drove them up and down Weymouth Front as if they were De Dion Boutons. Other, politer children were nervous of our reckless driving, especially the little boy and girl aged four and three who walked sedately beside their pretty nursemaid every morning. The nursemaid had an admirer who was probably unemployed as he used to meet her every morning and press his suit. One day as they sat in one of the shelters and he recited 'The Green Eye of the Little God' to her, we played at 'accidents' – pretending to run over the small children. We were beastly boys. As they ran away we drove after them and at them and in the end they fell weeping over the edge of the Front and onto the sand below – about four feet below. What a row that caused.

I don't remember if the nurse got the sack but the children were forbidden to speak to us and our car driving thereafter was severely restricted.

That was in 1922 and the little girl and I have been married since 1946.

Lance Percival
ENTERTAINER AND WRITER

When I was a macho nine-year-old and a resident of Timberscombe village in deepest Somerset, I fell in love with a girl called Isobel. Isobel lived on another planet, or to be exact, five miles away in Minehead. One evening, when I hinted to my mother that I might pay a courteous call on my Isobel sometime, the response was that I wasn't to even dream of doing such a ridiculous thing.

Ridiculous? My Isobel? I leapt on to my bike and pedalled furiously for the five long miles, even dodging an inquisitive policeman in Dunster. When I arrived at Isobel's home, I propped my bike up and gingerly rang the bell. What would her parents say? What if they answered the door?

The door opened and there was my true love in all her beautiful glory. 'Isobel', I shyly began, 'it's me, Lance'. 'Never heard of you' came the sharp reply, followed by a quick slam of the door.

The cycle ride home was the longest five miles I have ever known, and since I refused to admit failure to my mother, it was inconsolable tears at bedtime. The misery went on for a whole week, but suddenly lifted when my sister asked if I had ever met Isobel's identical twin sister!

Sir John Pilcher GCMG

FORMERLY H.M. AMBASSADOR TO THE PHILIPPINES, AUSTRIA AND JAPAN

I remember vividly a visit to a church in India in 1914 aged two. The atmosphere was serious in the extreme. When the curate arose to address us all, he spoke moving words about Greece. I must have heard Grease and understood its meaning. The contrast between grease and the solemnity of the occasion set me off in hoots of mirth. I was suppressed and removed and left the church, reverberating with my laughter. I have never thought mirth and religion to be incompatible.

Eileen Pollock

ACTRESS

My father taught me how to knit. How to cast on, and cast off, do plain stitch, and how to do purl. I'm not sure sticking your tongue sideways out of your mouth was part of his teaching, but I found it necessary. Knitting mattered. I aspired to being like my grandmother who knitted socks for the Irish missionaries in Africa – the nearer the Equator, the greater their courage, the thicker the socks. I couldn't wait to be seven, and in P2, where as soon as you got confirmed and had reached the use of reason, you got to knit squares for blankets for those selfsame Irish Missions.

In P2 I sat beside my best friend Mary, whose big sister Theresa was an air-hostess in Canada. I was so impressed I took Theresa as my Confirmation name, and when Mary said Theresa had taught her the Canadian stitch, I just had to learn it for my squares. Mary said: 'Well. You put the wool round three times like this, then you knit into the back, only you purl'. I tried, and failed and asked again. 'Look, you purl four together, right, then you wrap the wool round twice like this, and knit *back* into it with the other needle.' I must have looked confused. 'Eileen. Just take four stitches over, then wind the wool round five times, see? Then purl into the back of the next three, wrap the wool round, cast off two, and start again.' I still couldn't follow, I couldn't follow. 'Oh, just practice!'

Nothing in geometry could describe the results; algebra would be useless, and the latest computer graphics would refuse the data. My class and my teacher screamed with laughter. I didn't blame Mary, for after all she had been so patient (and *her* square had turned out fine). But I decided not to use my Confirmation name any more, and that I wouldn't be an air-hostess after all, in Canada or any other place.

The Rt. Hon. Lord Prior

FORMER POLITICIAN

My first letter home from school at the age of eight.

3rd May 1936

Dear Mummy and Daddy
Please send me a butterfly net tell daddy that I should like my other bat because I cannot find my other one, and I should like my stamp book and a little more money Please. I am going into the First Form. Pleas tell Nanny to plant out my Lettuces and to stick my sweet peas and to prick out my Pansies. Please send me a Fountain pen. Please tell nanny to right soon and to tell me about my garden. don't forget to send my bat
Please right soon Love many xxxxxxxxxxxxxxx From Jim

V.S. Pritchett CBE, FRSL
NOVELIST, SHORT STORY WRITER AND CRITIC

Yorkshire is the most loved of all the many places of my childhood. I was sent to my first school, the village school at the top of the town, up the lane from the Manse garden – it is just as it was when I was a child sixty years ago. The school sat in two classes and, I suppose, each class had about forty or fifty boys and girls, the girls in pinafores and long black or tan stockings. Douthwaite, Louthwaite, Thistlethwaite, Braithwaite, Branthwaite were the common surnames. The children spoke a dialect that was hard to understand. They came from farms and cottages, both sexes brisk and strenuous. We sat in three tiers in the class-room, the upper one for bigger children. While I was doing pothooks and capital D's from a script, the others were taught sums. Being a London child with a strange accent I began to swank, particularly to the girls. One who sat with me in the front offered to show me her belly if I lowered my own breeches. I did so, being anxious to show her my speciality – a blind navel, for the cord had been so cut that my navel was closed. In her opinion – and that of others – this was 'wrong' and foretold an early death because no air could get inside me. This distinction made me swank more. She did not keep her part of the bargain, neither did any of the other girls in Sedbergh. She put up her hand and told teacher. This was the first of many painful lessons, for I instantly loved girls.

Anneka Rice
TELEVISION PERSONALITY

One of my most vivid, haunting childhood memories is of a trip abroad – my first – when I was about eight. My family went skiing in Austria after months of collecting sixpences in a huge jar to finance the trip – I had never been in a plane before, let alone stayed in a hotel, so I was beside myself with excitement.

The holiday was a disaster. My father broke BOTH his legs on the first day, insisted on getting himself down the mountain and walking to the local doctor. He was then carted off in an ambulance to a big hospital many miles away to spend his holiday with plaster up to his thighs, lying flat on his back. He was only allowed out of hospital to travel home with us and we lost him and his wheelchair on a crowded railway platform. When we eventually arrived home in England after a fairly traumatic journey, we found we were locked out of the house at 4.00 a.m. I had nightmares about skiing and journeys for months afterwards!

I now make a living out of travelling and am constantly amazed that I ever got beyond that first trip! (It was certainly many, many years before I'd ever go near a ski slope!)

Sir Brian Rix CBE, DL

ACTOR AND CHAIRMAN OF MENCAP

Christmas 1935 was a great occasion for me – my first lead in the school play. I played Scout Napoleon Sharkey in *Nap's Adventure* which was really a crib from Ambrose Applejohn's *Adventure*. However, I was hardly conscious of plagiarism at that time, merely that I was able to overact to my heart's content. 'Avast, ye Lubbers' and other shouted orders were all part of the Second Act when I dreamt I was a pirate. Unfortunately, the shouting was a little dimmed by my usual loss of voice, but I got through somehow and was adjudged 'excellent' in the school review. Then followed two more years of Christmas bliss:

'In *The Rose and the Ring* Giglio was played by Rix (there's fame for you – none of your Christian-name rubbish) who thoroughly enjoyed his part and did it well.'

The same magazine contained another gem of information:

'The Swazi-Wallah Band, which was got up by Mr Gray and performed in the interval, was composed of the following – Mr Gray at the Piano, M. Strachan, B. Rix, A. Brown, W. Barr and W. Austin. Brown and Austin performed on the Bottle-Phone. The remainder played on their Kazoos and a remarkably good performance they gave.'

What with enjoying my part and giving a remarkably good performance on my kazoo – I must have been exhausted.

Sadly, 1937 was my last performance in a school play at St Bede's. 'In *He Found Adventure* the biggest part was taken by Brian Rix as Ian Stuart and a good job he made of it.' It was also my swan song at the school for the rest can be seen in the same magazine:

'Congratulations are due to the Rugger XV for its unbeaten season – no small achievement considering our numbers and those of our opponents. Congratulations are also due to Brian Rix who ended his successful cricket season last year by taking 8 wickets for 17 runs and scoring 54 not out when playing in a match organized in August by the Yorkshire CCC for E. Riding Schoolboys – in which match he was the youngest boy playing.' (My father nearly burst with pride that day – especially when the Bishop of Hull bestowed his apostolic blessing by saying I was the best boy cricketer he'd ever seen.)

Finally, in March: *Ave Atque Vale –*

'B.N.R. Rix, Head Boy, XI (Colours), XV (Colours), VIII (Colours) – to Bootham School, York.'

Robert Robinson

RADIO AND TELEVISION PRESENTER

The best – and rudest – school report I ever saw (I wish it had been mine) read, simply, 'Eats and cheats'.

Lord Romsey

OWNER OF BROADLANDS. FILM, TELEVISION AND
RADIO ENTREPRENEUR

It was a beautiful warm summer's day, the sort of summer we never seem to have any more. I remember the enjoyment of running on the luscious green lawn, in and out of flower beds filled with delicious smells and covered in strange objects which hummed and buzzed. I stopped and stared at a sight I had never before seen. These objects seemed to hang in the air and move with amazing grace and beauty. I turned and tripped and fell sprawling in the warm grass, I lay there for a second dazed and, simultaneously, became aware of a beautiful, large brown and honey-coloured bird writhing beside me on the ground. At the same time, a terrible pain struck my hand, pain I had never felt before. I picked myself up as best I could and ran, staggering, to where my parents were sitting under a striped umbrella. I was two years old, I had had my first – unhappy – meeting with bees. Perhaps strangely, nearly forty years later, they remain my favourite creatures.

Sir Archibald Ross KCMG

FORMER H.M. AMBASSADOR

About the time of my third birthday my mother, who had to rejoin my father, a District and Sessions Judge in India, left me in the care of my godmother, who lived in Clifton. Several of the houses nearby took in Belgian refugees. I prayed for 'Servia and all our Allies'. Sitting in my pram under the trees, I regaled admiring adults with extracts from the *Morning Post*, prefaced by the words: 'It says in the paper today'.

I was thus destined from an early age to play the Pedant and the Prig; and these characters stood me in good stead throughout my professional life. Thanks to the first, my ideas, though sometimes unimaginative and not seldom erroneous, were dressed in so exact and elegant a prose as to be instantly intelligible even to my official superiors, while the writings of others, unable to express themselves clearly, would throw me into a purensy and force me to apply the surgery of the pen to the slightest irregularity of style or grammar. The second, masked by a condescension necessary in changing circumstances, required me nevertheless to observe the injunction of Talleyrand: never to cease for one moment in the twenty-four hours of the day to be the Ambassador of my Country.

The Rt. Hon. the Lord St John of Fawsley FRSL

**AUTHOR, CHAIRMAN OF THE ROYAL FINE ARTS COMMISSION
AND FORMER CABINET MINISTER**

I used to be taken regularly for an airing in Hyde Park in my perambulator by a series of nannies, none of whom, for reasons which elude me, remained very long in our employment. However, I remember a particularly delightful Irish girl who placed her handbag in the perambulator at the beginning of the Broad Walk, I would then throw the handbag out on to the Walk, whereupon she would pick it up and replace it in exactly the same place. Following this I would throw it out again and so the whole delightful process would continue until we reached the end of the walk and I was taken out of the perambulator. No exercise in later life has ever given me such joy. The combination of excitement at throwing the handbag out and knowing with complete moral certainty that it would be returned and I could throw it out again gave me a foretaste of Heaven. This, I thought in suitably childish terms, is what eternity will be like.

Peter de Savary

ENTREPRENEUR

I began sailing when I was eight years old. One of my earliest experiences happened when I was sailing in the Solent with my brothers.

My parents had taken us there for the day with my godparents and they were very keen to watch us sail. While we were at sea a storm came up and our boat capsized. Fortunately, a rescue helicopter was on hand and we were all retrieved safely.

In spite of this incident, I have always loved the sea and sailing.

Jimmy Savile OBE
VOLUNTARY HOSPITAL WORKER

'Don't call us, we'll call you' is the famous showbiz brushoff. I claim to be the youngest recipient of this award, at the age of two, and from the Big Agent Himself, the Good Lord!

Actually at not quite two years old I was dying. The Master, or one of his minders, hearing of this imminent addition to his heavenly host, sent in the nick of time a miracle cure.

After some years of a strange life and several occasions when I could have quite easily died, and nearly did, it gradually dawned on me that the Good Lord is as determined not to have me join his heavenly army as I am apparently determined to enlist. Some babies are born strong, some weak. Being the youngest of seven it would appear that my father's last effort was lacking in the juices of strength. Eye-witnesses have it that I was born sound asleep.

Much love and care sustained my shrimplike form until finally, anointed with the oils of the last rites and resembling one of Mr Skipper's excellent sardines, my maternal grandma lowered a mirror over my mouth to catch the bloom of the last breath. My mama, who was to become famous as 'the Duchess' and my only real true love to date, was in Leeds Cathedral offering a prayer of intercession to a then unknown but hopefully possible saint, Margaret Sinclair. At that precise moment my grandma collected not the last breath but a right eyeful of involuntary, well aimed pee. I have continued to pee on the Establishment ever since with similar success.

Lt. Col. Sir James Scott Bt.
LORD LIEUTENANT OF HAMPSHIRE

I can recall a conversation with my mother when I was aged six. Mother said, 'Who are you most fond of?' I replied, 'Bogie (the mule).'

Mother, slightly disappointed asked 'and who are you next most fond of?'

'Mr Smith who looks after Bogie.'

The result was a rather disappointed mother.

Sir Peter Scott CH, CBE, DSC, FRS

**FOUNDER CHAIRMAN OF THE WORLDWIDE FUND FOR
NATURE AND FOUNDER OF THE WILDFOWL TRUST**

One of my two godfathers was Admiral Sir Clements Markham, President of the Royal Geographical Society at the time of my father's first expedition. It was he who had selected my father to lead it, and it was for him that I was christened with the middle name of Markham. My second godfather was the Scottish playwright Sir James Barrie, who had met my father in 1905, soon after he returned from his first Antarctic expedition in the *Discovery*. For all the time that I knew him, Barrie lived on the top floor of Adelphi Terrace House, overlooking the river. The room in which he wrote was dominated by a huge open hearth piled high with wood ash, and with a high-backed settle in the inglenook on one side of it. The room, so far as I recall, was scarcely altered at all in the twenty-five years that I knew it. It was full of pipe smoke and books. As a very small boy I used to go there for tea, sometimes with my mother, sometimes alone and feeling very independent. There is no doubt that Barrie knew all about how to get on with children. Although there were often long silences I cannot ever remember feeling shy in his company. He wrote delightful comic letters, often in rhyme, and always full of invention.

He once took me to *Peter Pan* and we sat in a box. Having seen the play several times since, I cannot now remember what impression it made upon me this first time. I was, after all, only four-and-a-half years old. But Barrie always described how he asked me in the taxi on the way home which part I had enjoyed the most. 'I think,' I am supposed to have said, after some deliberation, 'that I enjoyed it most when I dropped the programme on the fat lady's head in the interval.'

Terry Scott

ACTOR

I don't know how old I was, but I shall never ever forget having to go to school and tell the teacher I couldn't go swimming, because Mum said my costume wasn't aired!

Childhood Memories

Ned Sherrin

PRODUCER, DIRECTOR, WRITER AND PRESENTER

A green field covered in cowslips. A small boy just over two years old. An indulgent aunt. Together they pick the flowers until the boy is bored. The aunt demurs. The boy surveys the carpet of cowslips and says with awful cuteness, 'We must leave some for another little boy to pick for his mother.'

I have been told this story so many times that I now believe that it is my earliest memory. However, it is no longer possible to distinguish between the event and the account . . . and my infant instinct to find an excuse for going home which would leave me in a better light rings true – in the light of later developments.

The green field lay between the villages of High Ham and Low Ham, on part of my father's farm, Gawler's Farm in Somerset. We left it in 1934 when I was three.

Two more authentic memories. The first visit to the new farmhouse still occupied by the previous tenant – tears and disgrace. Then, moving into the new home which was much larger, an old coaching inn at Kingweston. I ran lost around the unfamiliar stone passages crying, 'Mummy, where is I? I's lost.' The dialogue is perhaps too fey to be true and the grammar may have deteriorated in the years of indulgent retelling; but that is how I recall it.

The village of Kingweston as I became aware of it was still feudally organized. The squire, Captain W.E. Dickinson (suddenly OBE during the war – for organizing local knitting for the troops: as they said in the village, ' 'Ee be OBE, 'ee be'), trained as an architect and was, as far as I could see, occupied entirely in watercolour painting, amateur theatricals and fierce readings of the lessons in church on Sundays with scant regard to punctuation. He was thin and later bent. Mrs Dickinson was ample and cloaked, in my memory, in long businesslike but flowing suits of blue or brown. Miss Dickinson was the older of two children – a tall, shy girl. The son and heir was Caleb, handsome, charming, fair and fresh-faced, apparently ill at ease with the restrictions of Kingweston life and keen to be one of the boys. In the background, sinister so it seemed through my father's eyes, loomed the stumpy, sturdy figure of Miss Buckle, the children's governess, who stayed on, he asserted, simply to meddle in village business.

119

David Shilling
INTERNATIONAL HAT DESIGNER

I never had a bicycle as a child. My pride and joy was a model yacht that came from Harrods, all pristine white hull, sails and rigging – until one day I dropped a jelly on it – I don't mean just a bit but a whole zonking great blackcurrant rabbit – and it was never quite the same again. Now I'm always the first to feel sick at sea and that's apparently the sign of a good sailor!

No! I never did have a bicycle but I did have a three-wheeler – three full size wheels and rather stately with a whicker basket on the front. I've never since learned to balance well on a bike and when I left school I had a racing tricycle built to get to work on, with eight-speed gears and all the extras! At Lloyd's garage they charged 50p for parking cars – but 10p for cycles – so I paid 15p as I had three wheels. It felt great racing Ferraris down the Euston Road and beating them through the traffic and paying less than a third to park the thing – but in the end I became defeated by fear of Hyde Park Corner.

Dennis Silk JP, MA
WARDEN OF RADLEY COLLEGE, OXFORD

It all started with a game of hide and seek. It was Sunday evening and my father, who was assistant curate at St Mary the Virgin, Primrose Hill, had gone off to take evensong. We four children had done our stint at Matins. We now had free range of the house and there was no adult anywhere to be seen to intrude on our glorious game.

As the youngest of the four and a mere five-year-old I was wildly excited and eager to show my paces to my brother and sisters. Having been very swiftly discovered on the first two occasions I decided to go for a real 'secret' place and persuaded my brother to open the large bottom drawer of a big tallboy, which had lost its handles. This he did with difficulty, in I climbed and he duly pushed the drawer shut. I barely fitted and within seconds I was regretting my decision. The drawer was tightly sealed and I could barely breathe. The sweat began to roll down my forehead. I was so tightly constricted I could barely move my hands and feet, let alone turn over. The feeling of claustrophobia was overpowering.

Soon I was screaming to be released, but to open a now heavy drawer with no handles was beyond the power of my eight-year-old brother. They soon became as terrified as I. Halfway to unconsciousness I could hear them scrabbling at the outside of the drawer, but to no avail. My screams became fainter and fainter. I could feel the waves of unconsciousness washing over me.

My father's sermon that night was fortunately shorter than usual. Arriving home he found his children in a hysterical state. He was taken at a gallop to the tallboy from which all sounds had ceased to emanate. Swiftly but with some difficulty, he prised the drawer open and found his limp, semi-conscious younger son, purple in the face but alive. That same young son still has nightmares about premature burial and games of hide and seek.

Carmen Silvera
ACTRESS

On my seventh birthday I had a lesson on never being jealous of others. At my party one little girl fainted and was cradled in my grandmother's arms until she recovered. My Grandma Silvera, who was visiting us from Canada, was a shy, reserved lady, not easily given to displays of affection and I simply couldn't bear seeing her being so attentive to someone else – so I promptly decided to faint myself in order to get a cuddle. The wise old lady realized what I had done and the reason behind it – so she gently took me in her arms and carried me to my room and there told me how much she loved me and I need never resort to deception or be jealous of anyone for there would always be someone who would think I was special. Her gentle but loving reproach was the lesson of a lifetime that I have struggled to remember ever since.

Donald Sinden CBE, FRSA

ACTOR

The village of Ditchling in Sussex before the Second World War: glorious years of sunshine days; the roads (in my memory) were as wide as the M1 with rarely a car to be seen; climbing to the top of Ditchling Beacon – or more frequently to the top of Lodge Hill; the annual Gooseberry Show and the attendant Fair; November the 11th when men from the butchers, bakers, grocers, chemists would transform themselves and parade bemedalled to the War Memorial and a lonely bugler would eek out the Last Post; and bespoke coffins were made by the village carpenter behind the forge where the blacksmith shod enormous horses to the smell of sizzling hooves.

Valerie Singleton

TELEVISION JOURNALIST AND PRESENTER

The school was in a private house which appeared to have a corridor that ran from the front door straight to the back of the house, where a few iron steps led down into the garden. In the garden I remember there was a huge climbing frame – well, it certainly seemed huge to a four-year-old.

The classroom was in a room towards the back of the house on the left of the corridor. It was a study with a big, round table in it which filled the room. The pupils sat round the table and I began to bang the leg of the table with my foot, despite being told repeatedly to stop it. I was being deliberately provocative.

I don't know how long this went on for before the teacher lost patience, but eventually, as punishment, I was moved across the corridor to the room on the other side. Like the corridor, this room ran from the front to the back of the house and was obviously not used very often, as every single piece of furniture was covered in a dust sheet and all was gloomy and frightening.

Terrified, I crouched behind one of the armchairs with my arms over my head and my eyes tight shut. I don't know how long it was before I heard the voice of the teacher saying to my mother, who had come to collect me, 'She's been a very naughty little girl. We've had to punish her.'

The Rev. the Lord Soper MA

METHODIST MINISTER, CHRISTIAN SOCIALIST AND PACIFIST

Wright's Coal Tar Soap is an excellent cleaning agent, but for me it is very much more than that. It is a magic carpet which transports me to the land of my childhood or, more particularly, to its holidays. Wave a bar of this soap in front of my nose and I am immediately reliving holiday experiences from more than seventy years ago. A whiff of it and memories come flooding in.

At the beginning of August in those far-off days the Soper family took itself by train to Minehead. When we arrived at the boarding house my mother understandably thought that we needed cleaning up a bit. Out came a bar of Wright's Coal Tar Soap, and the world of my childhood still floods back whenever I catch its nostalgic aroma with an immediacy which is Proustian but much more simple.

Usually we travelled down to Devon on the first Saturday in August and, believe it or not, the very first excursion we made was not down to the sea but to discover the whereabouts of the Methodist Church. If we were to begin our holiday properly on the first day, which was also the first day of the week, then Sunday observance came before holiday activities. Such was the quality and aroma of those holidays, renewed and as vital now as they were then. Though perhaps I ought to add that the strict Sabbatarian discipline which would not allow us to go bathing on Sunday no longer carries the same absolute requirements as it did then.

In one sense the holiday began on the Monday. The unpacking of the trunk had begun on the Saturday night. For most of the year this tin box played no part in my life, but about a fortnight before the holiday began it appeared in our front room at home and the ceremony of filling it began. Each of us three children was allowed to contribute, but not too much. Nevertheless it still amazes me as to what in fact found its way into that trunk. When full to bursting, it was roped up and a card was put in the front window inviting Carter Paterson to take it to Minehead. It always seemed a little short of miraculous that when we arrived there the trunk had preceded us and was sitting in our diggings.

Then down to the beach complete with what was quite correctly called a collapsible tent. This structure was composed of a number of parts and my father was responsible for assembling them. We were enrolled as assistants and all the more enthusiastic to see it erected, because only then could we get into our bathing costumes and test the water. The assembly of the tent was by no means easy. My father was indomitable. I once remember him saying that he'd get that wretched tent up if it was the last thing he did! Which even now has an almost apocalyptic ring to it. We took it in turns to undress inside it and thence into the sea – *en famille.*

If swimming and basking in the sun (and it seemed to shine most of the time in those far-off days) and playing ball games filled most of the day, the high spot of the evening was the band stand where Uncle Mac's concert party presided. Its initial attraction was that you did not have to pay to go in – it was a free for all out of doors and I found it irresistible. I wonder how many who may read these words remember 'The pretty little girl from Nowhere' which was one of Uncle Mac's most popular hits. My father recollected the words, my brother, my sister and I reproduced the tune and we played it and sang it on the boarding-house piano, whereafter it became part of our musical repertoire at home. I daresay it infringed copyright but it was a constant and happy reminder of the concert party and its genuine delights.

Those were the days that the whiff of a bar of soap revitalize so long after they happened, and with an immediacy which destroys the passage of time. 'Time like an ever rolling stream,' says the hymn, 'bears all its sons away.' This is true inasmuch as we are mortal beings and our earthly span is strictly limited but when the hymn goes on to assert that we, or our years, 'fly forgotten as a dream dies at the opening day' – I beg to differ. A simple sense, such as the sense of smell can preserve and so re-enact the past and enable us mortals to enjoy something of eternity.

Sir Greville Spratt

CHAIRMAN OF ACTION RESEARCH FOR THE CRIPPLED CHILD

Was it really that long ago? Why is it that I can remember the names of all those that stood and sat beside the five-year-old with the shock of blonde hair in the school photo and yet I sometimes forget the surname of my tennis partner or perhaps even fleetingly my host's Christian name escapes me.

The incredibly long walk to school which was all of half a mile, two roads to cross with one hand firmly grasped leaving the other in the interim to play upon the Golf Club railings with a stick in seemingly melodious fashion for all to appreciate.

Oh the problems – the fear of Thursdays when a real live Master took us for General Knowledge and replaced our gentle lady teachers who never called us by our surnames. The ordeal of Prayers at nine o'clock when we the Juniors marched in and the Senior Boys in long trousers haughty and tall sniggered at our shorts and if we were out of step. The accidents if the Headmaster spoke too long and our nerves gave way so that the emergency clothing store had discreetly to be utilized. One never forgets your first love: the music teacher who played the xylophone and taught us 'There is a green hill far away' and then doubled up as Akela helping us do up our back buttons with cut braces – once I even held her hand.

What happy memories that will always linger on though the old stone buildings have gone and a modern housing estate stands there instead.

Chris Tarrant

RADIO PRESENTER

When you're a kid, because you've had little or no chance to travel around and compare your experiences with other kids outside your immediate circle of playmates and schoolfriends, you tend to assume that everybody else's lives and habits are identical to your own. If there are a dozen kids out of twenty in your class who all breed rattlesnakes for pets and come to school on white rhinos, you must naturally assume that that's about the national average. Nobody ever tells you you're in a nuthouse.

Well, it was the same for me with Finger Flicking. I just assumed that that was what everybody else was doing all over the world, or certainly all over the British Isles.

It was all Mr Wormwell's fault. Or Major Wormwell as he insisted on being called at least twenty years after the cessation of all hostilities, and in any case I've had a lot of doubts since about whether he actually ever went anywhere more dangerous than Basingstoke. Anyway, the Major was the Headmaster of this very twee little school that my mum and dad decided to pack me off to as soon as I was big enough to see over a desk and sit on a lavatory without a serious risk of drowning. And it was on that first day at school that the Major initiated me in Finger Flicking. What basically happened was that he announced something like 'as this is the first day of term you can all have this afternoon off,' and all the six- and seven-year-olds all round me started waving their arms in the air like helicopters. Even the Major joined in. Apparently it was what you did at school when you were pleased about something. To define it more precisely you touch the thumb and middle finger of each hand together, and then, with the rest of your fingers splayed open and your elbows bent so that your hands are about level with your shoulders, you wave your hands back and forth from the wrist as fast as possible. (It comes at this point in reading this book that you get odd looks from people sitting all around you and probably get asked to go and sit somewhere else.) The noise when done by a whole school of children at morning assembly can be deafening, but at my nice little school it happened a lot. Sometimes if the news just brought delight to one individual, he would stand there happily flicking away all on his own. No embarrassment whatsoever. It was just what you did.

'Well done, Tarrant, you're only just turned nine and you've got all three letters right in "CAT".'

'Thank you, sir.' Flick Flick Flick.

We all did it at the slightest hint of happiness, indeed until I was twelve I flicked two or three times a week sometimes on my own, sometimes with just a couple of close friends, sometimes with the whole school and the Headmaster. Naturally I assumed that this was going on all over British classrooms at the same time. I mean I didn't know Major Wormwell was completely out of his mind, did I?

Shaw Taylor

RADIO AND TELEVISION PRESENTER

My love of the sea began on the murky waters of the Pool of London . . . seven o'clock on a summer's Saturday morning . . . alongside Tower Pier the gleaming hull of the *Royal Eagle* bound for Ramsgate with Woolwich, Southend and Margate as ports of call. On the wing of the bridge the impressive bearded figure of Captain Braithwaite . . . just a nod fore and aft, the ropes thrown, and the swish of the churning paddles taking her away downstream. Looking out for Uncle John coming aboard at Woolwich . . . and the craftily slipped florin into the hand of the chief engineer that had me standing over the hissing pistons in the gleaming engine room, waiting for the clang of the bell that would signal Captain Braithwaite's command on the engine-room telegraph. Ashore at Ramsgate Harbour and a week of bliss, but always knowing that on Saturday evening I would be back on board the *Royal Eagle* as she ploughed her way back up the Thames. The silhouette of Tower Bridge against the moon as the ship's intercom begins to play 'Open up them pearly gates' and a hundred or more Cockney voices join in the chorus. Majestically the sponsons of the bridge rise and the *Eagle* steams beneath them to tie up at Tower Pier . . . until next year!

Norman Thelwell

ILLUSTRATOR

I don't remember being born, nor anything else until I was somewhere in my third year. No doubt I had conversed with my mother many times before but the first full conversation I can clearly recall took place when my Auntie Margaret was present. They were standing in our kitchen, arms folded, talking about whatever grown-ups talked about.

'What can I draw, Mam?' Either she didn't hear me or she found the question too tedious to deal with at that moment. I pulled at her skirt.

'What can I draw, Mam?'

'Draw a motor car,' she said and went on talking to Auntie.

'I've drawn a motor car . . .'

'Well draw a boat.'

'I've drawn a boat.'

'Draw a house then!'

'I've drawn a house . . .' . . . 'Mam! I've drawn a house.'

'Oh for goodness sake, child! Go and draw yourself.'

It was the first time I had come face to face with a brilliant idea. I went away instantly and made a drawing of myself. I don't remember how long it took me but it was obviously far less time than my mother had hoped. I had to drag at her skirt several times before she looked down. She took my piece of paper, made another point or two to my Auntie, glanced at my drawing and looked stunned. She handed the scrap of paper back to me as if it were hot.

'What did you want to draw yourself doing that for?' she said.

'Let me see Norm,' said Auntie, taking my self-portrait. She turned her face away instantly making strangled little sobs. I think she was laughing at something.

'Kids!' said my mother. 'Who'd have 'em?'

It was my first lesson in the power of the visual arts.

Major General Julian Thompson
CB, OBE
COMMANDED THE COMMANDO BRIGADE
IN THE FALKLANDS CAMPAIGN

Schooldays

Prep school in England; what a culture-shock after boarding school in Kashmir. Instead of a three-day train journey across pre-partition India from Calcutta to Rawalpindi, followed by a two-day bus journey to Srinagar; a mere three hours from Waterloo. A compartment full of pink-faced strangers, instead of a four-berth sleeper shared with chums; a train with no corridor; over a hundred boys by the time we reached Delhi, and one master to control us all! Swarming out when the train stopped at stations, day or night; jinking round porters hurrying through the crowd with trunks on their heads, hopping over recumbent bodies, buying the lurid sweetmeats off the vendors' trays, ignoring the silent voice; 'Don't eat anything from the stalls at the stations, Darling.' Grubby little boys, mostly in shorts and shirts, but a few hopeful show-offs in baggy 1940s ski pants and jackets, despite the eighty degree midday cold weather temperature; after all there might be snow in Srinagar, and certainly in Gulmarg. Pity the three boys in whose compartment the master made a fourth. Not for them the delight of pelting the waiting passengers at through stations with oranges, or dowsing

Above: Alan Titchmarsh aged two with his
grandfather's fox terrier, Smudgie
Below: Sir Michael Tippett (right) with his
mother and younger brother in 1908

Above: Simon Williams, aged three
Right: Sir David Willcocks as a young chorister at the Westminster Abbey Choir School
       : Susannah York (right) with her mother and elder sister

them with water from the jug so thoughtfully provided by the railway company, or holding midnight feasts of soda pop, dhal and rice. Hanging out of the window, with an eyeful of smuts as we clanked over some great bridge, the river far below shining in the moonlight. Exchanging backchat with soldiers bound for the Burma battles on a troop-train halted on a siding opposite.

Riding our bikes into school a couple of miles from our house, the cold nipping our noses and ears. In the summer, paddling canoes and sailing on the Dhal and Wular lakes. Who can climb down the anchor chain of the houseboat and sit on the bottom of the lake so that the house-matron starts panicking? What a hope, she's seen it all. Climbing to the 15,000-foot summit of Mahadeo in nailed sandals, with the 'squits'; 'probably last night's vegetable curry', diagnoses some ten-year-old expert.

Christopher Timothy

ACTOR

In 1948 or 1949, I can't remember which . . . I was taken to my first pantomime at the theatre in Hammersmith; it starred Jimmy Jewel and Ben Warris and I think it was *Babes In The Wood*, but I can't remember that either!

One of the 'props' was a big, narrow, yellowy thing, about ten feet in length and I asked someone what it was . . . 'It's a *banana*,' was the reply. The show was wonderful and it started my lifelong passion for pantomime.

Sometime later, months even, my grandmother returned from shopping and she seemed excited; 'Surprise' she whispered 'I've got some bananas'. I was amazed; I hardly dared ask . . . 'Er . . . how *many*?' and Gran replied, quite casually, 'About six, I think'.

Incredulously I enquired 'Where *are* they?' 'In the kitchen' Gran answered, smiling broadly. How can she be so matter-of-fact, I thought, as I dashed down the passage and threw open the kitchen door. But where were they? Two or three bulging brown paper bags, of average size, sat on the table . . . but nothing that could possibly contain six bananas, which I now knew to be a huge fruit about ten feet long!

My first sight of the *real thing* was a disappointment, my first *taste* started my *other* passion . . . for bananas.

Alan Titchmarsh
GARDENER, WRITER AND BROADCASTER

I have very fond memories of my Grandad Hardisty, on my mother's side. It was he who unwittingly introduced me to gardening on his allotment when I was very small. He had an old toolshed full of seeds and ancient gardening tools, rhubarb that he drenched with soot water and blackberries scrambling over brass bedsteads. I can remember walking with him – me in my baggy dungarees and he in his collarless shirt, waistcoat with Albert and soft trilby hat, hand in hand through his pea sticks hung with cocoa tins to frighten away the birds. His was the first dog I ever encountered – Smudgie was her name. She was a smooth-haired Fox Terrier and had her own very special tricks. She could sit up and 'knit' with her front paws! None of my Labradors has ever been able to do that.

Sir John Tooley
FORMER GENERAL DIRECTOR OF THE
ROYAL OPERA HOUSE

Some of my happiest memories of childhood are centred around summer holidays. For many years my parents rented a house at Herne Bay for the month of August. It was one of those seaside houses constructed of wood, and sited very close to the beach which was reached by a short flight of steps.

The entire household moved to Herne Bay for this annual holiday. A lorry was hired to carry bed linen, provisions and all the paraphernalia for a month away. In the lorry travelled cook, nanny and a maid, together with cook's mother who came to lend a hand in the running of the house. My mother and father went by car or by train, but naturally I preferred to travel in the lorry with my brother.

The excitement was colossal as we left home and even greater as the sea came into sight. Not a moment was lost in getting into the sea and, encouraged by my mother, who was a ferocious swimmer, we did so in all weathers.

These were idyllic holidays, mostly spent on the beach and in or on the sea. Sailing became an early pastime and fishing off the pier or from a boat gave added variety.

Other entertainment was provided by Punch and Judy shows, dodgems, band concerts, concert parties on the pier and, as a very special treat, rides in a speedboat. These were all very much part of English seaside life in the late 1920s and while they may have lacked some of the sophistication of today's holidays they certainly made up for it in many other ways.

Meriel Tufnell MBE

FIRST LADY JOCKEY UNDER JOCKEY CLUB RULES

Having been born with dislocated hips, and a chronic asthmatic, riding was easier than walking at the beginning. I started to ride at around four and to walk at four and a half.

My father was in the Royal Navy and we were posted to such places as Japan and Australia, for two years at a time, travelling the world each time to get there. Living in Australia at the age of eleven, must be every little girl's dream. As a lover of animals more than people, that country has to be the greatest. We came in close contact with so many exotic and wonderful creatures. We managed to tame quite a lot of the wild ones – e.g. kangaroos, cockatoos, equanas, kookaburras, plus of course the more dangerous animals of sharks, snakes and spiders.

Their horse shows were quite unlike ours. They would start at seven a.m. and finish at ten p.m. With grown men doing gymkhana races such as our flag races here, bull-dogging, bronco riding, milking the cow, steer riding and many other wonderful events – going on under floodlights well into the night. Those have got to be some of the best times of my life.

This meant my education was to be a stream of governesses! What appalling creatures they are! I still have one who lives in Canada and keeps in constant touch. However, the rest were out of a book! I remember one occasion while my mother was interviewing one of these monsters! We had sat down for a really pompous lunch, when three little piglets, dashed through the dining-room, under the table, and out through the French windows. While my mother tried hard to convince the old hag that this never usually happens, I (wicked child as I was) tried hard to convince her it would happen daily! She didn't take the position!!

Childhood Memories

The Rev. Dr Chad Varah OBE, MA

FOUNDER OF THE SAMARITANS

The Day I Burnt down the School Lab.

I am never likely to forget this day, some time in 1928, because I was birched for my offence. Hundreds of boys had been *caned* – I had even, as a prefect, occasionally caned a misbehaving boy in my dormitory – but no one in living memory had been birched. It was well known that if you were birched, on your bare bottom, a notice stating how many strokes had to be posted on the board and signed by the Headmaster. This enabled you to charge sixpence a look on bath night.

Of course, I didn't burn down the lab. The last time I visited Worksop College, in the Dukeries in Sherwood Forest, it was still there. So how come there was this prestigeful notice?

> Varah, E.C.
> For burning down the chemistry laboratory.
> 6 strokes of the Birch.
> Signed, F.J. Shirley, Headmaster?

As he's now dead, you'll have to take my word for it that I was doing extra work in my own time ('Yah, dirty swot' – but those who sneered thus were happy to have a half-holiday when I got my scholarship at Oxford) and needed some white phosphorus. This, in sticks like yellow candles, was kept in a jar under water, as it ignited spontaneously on exposure to the air. I fished out a stick with tongs, cut off a piece the size of a pea, and the rest of the stick shot across the lab. and began to emit clouds of white smoke on the tiled floor, where it melted into a puddle. The smoke, Phosphorus pentoxide, poured out of the windows, and the fire brigade came. They wouldn't listen to my instructions, so they and the various masters trod in the stuff and spread it all over the school. Even in the organ loft in chapel you never knew when there'd be a slight bang and a puff of smoke. As this continued for the rest of term, I guess six strokes were a small price to pay. Don't tell anyone, but birching hurts less than caning.

Kenneth Waller

ACTOR

Early Influences: My primary schoolteacher, Miss Orchard at Hythe (Hampshire) Junior School. She made me play the piano for morning prayers and wouldn't let me change the music until I could play it perfectly. We had 'Daisies are our Silver' for a whole term.

My English teacher, Miss Agnes Graham at Brockenhurst Grammar School who made Shakespeare fun. Our weekly visits to the Grand Theatre, Southampton, where between the ages of five and eleven I saw everything from *Macbeth* to *While Parents Sleep*.

Early Triumphs: My appearances with my mother's concert party. I was dressed in a white velvet suit and recited epics such as 'I Had a Penny' by A.A. Milne all over the New Forest to TUMULTUOUS APPLAUSE! Winning 1st Prize at the Southampton Musical Competition for ten- to eleven-year-olds in 1937. Winning the School Integrity Prize.

Early Disaster: My first Christmas Play at Junior School. I recited a verse and then fastened a bauble onto the Christmas Tree – two minutes later it fell off and smashed to smithereens. I cried and was inconsolable.

First Memory: My mother playing the 'Moonlight Sonata'.

First Pets: Very unfortunate experiences – my cat Sooty was stolen by the soldiers who were camped in the field behind our house in the early days of the Second World War. My dog Patch who was accidentally killed by a motor-bike, driven by my father's best friend. My goldfish which froze during an unexpectedly cold spell.

Baroness Warnock

MISTRESS OF GIRTON COLLEGE, CAMBRIDGE

A portrait of my grandfather, Sir Felix Schuster Bt., now broods over the fireplace of my flat in Girton, bearded, substantial, a drooping left eyelid giving his face an air of accusing melancholy. He was a banker. His family came to England from Frankfurt when he was a small child, converting from Judaism to

133

Christianity soon after. (His rather large christening robes were used for my children and grandchildren. It wasn't till quite recently that I realized that he must have been a stocky two-year-old when the broderie-anglaise gown was first used.) He always spoke with a noticeable German accent.

My first memory of him was one of the times he came to stay in Winchester with my widowed mother, his eldest daughter, who was terrified of him. I was, I suppose, about five, and she warned me, along with my older brother and sisters 'Do try to remember whatever you do not to speak to Grandpapa about the Gold Standard'.

We used to be taken to stay with him and my Aunt Evelyn, unmarried and devoted to his care, in his house in West Sussex, where he came down from London to hold shooting parties and musical soirées. He instructed us in music; indeed we had to play our piano pieces to him on the grand piano in the library (usually hornpipies and rigadoons from an admirable series called *Easy Classics: Purcell*). But he told us that there was no one to be admired except Bach, Beethoven and Brahms. Once, much later, at school I nearly fainted with emotion when I heard, for the first time since those days, the particular Beethoven sonata he used to play for our instruction (opus 31 no. 2). He was a good, tragic, dashing pianist, and played a lot of chamber music, as well as his endless solitary Beethoven.

Sometimes he demanded that we should go for walks with him, round the farms that were part of the estate (now belonging to ICI). We were got ready at least half an hour too early, for fear of keeping him waiting. One time he asked us (me and my sister next older than me) what were our favourite colours. My sister, a much more candid and open child than I, said 'green'. I, seeking to impress, said 'black'; upon which my grandfather took his stick and slashed at the corn growing by the side of the track and shouted 'never, NEVER let me hear you say that BLACK is a COLOUR!' I was completely horrified. I thought I had uttered an obscenity, mentioned one of the things which, as we were aware, must mysteriously not be mentioned. Luckily, only my loyal sister had heard me, and thereafter neither of us liked to speak of it, either to each other or anyone else.

All the same, the first fictional figure I ever fell seriously in love with was Jo's German professor in *Little Women*. He, sheltering her under his umbrella, was undoubtedly my grandfather.

The Rt. Hon. Bernard Weatherill MP

SPEAKER OF THE HOUSE OF COMMONS

This poem hung in my father's bedroom and whenever, as a child, my sisters or I said we could not do something, we were always required to repeat the poem.

Somebody Said It Couldn't Be Done

Somebody said that it couldn't be done
But he with a chuckle replied
That maybe it couldn't, but he would be one
Who wouldn't say so till he'd tried.
So he buckled right in with the trace of a grin
On his face – If he worried he hid it.
He started to sing as he tackled the thing
That couldn't be done, and he did it!

Somebody scoffed, Oh you'll never do that
At least no one ever has done it,
But he took off his coat, and he took off his hat
And the first thing we knew he'd begun it.
With a lift of his chin, and a bit of a grin,
Without any doubting or quiddit,
He started to sing as he tackled the thing
That couldn't be done, and he did it.

There are thousands to tell you it cannot be done.
There are thousands to prophesy failure.
There are thousands to point out to you one by one
The dangers that wait to assail you.
But just buckle in with a bit of a grin.
Just take off your coat and go to it.
Just start in to sing as you tackle the thing
That cannot be done, and you'll do it!

The Duke of Westminster

At my private school I spent my entire waking hours thinking and playing football. I was perhaps the idlest centre-forward ever to grace a football field, but still hold, as far as I know, the goal-scoring record, having the ability to kick extremely straight and very hard with both feet. Clearly my studies suffered as a result and in exasperation my headmaster in his end of term report wrote 'This boy has more brains in his feet than he has in his head'!

Sam Whitbread DL

CHAIRMAN OF WHITBREAD AND COMPANY

A Sixteen-Year-Old's First Flight, January 1954

At about 5.45 a.m. we were herded into a coach. Some of my fellow travellers were wearing exotic ski outfits; others, rather smart clothes. I struck what I thought was a happy medium by wearing grey flannels, tweed coat and ski boots. Nearly everybody was in a party and I got a seat to myself. We went through Staines, Egham, Sunningdale and Camberley and at about 7 o'clock drew into Blackbushe Airport, shrouded in mist.

We got out and went into the main building, which was quite long but with only one floor. A rather cold airhostess with a very determined jaw snapped, 'Move straight into the buffet, please'. We obeyed without a murmur.

Our meal began with a few cornflakes. I say 'a few' and I mean it, for the airport caterers might have counted them there were so few. Four spoonfuls of cornflakes did little more than bias ourselves against the airline breakfast. However, our hopes were raised when a large plate of bacon, eggs and sausages was placed before us by a female of amazon build and temperament. We tucked into this with a will, together with tea which was stirred with a communal spoon.

Just as we were finishing our banquet, there was a noise behind me like a sawmill and there stood the square-chinned hostess demanding our 'passenger service charge of five shillings'. I was prepared and paid her two dirty half-crowns.

Suddenly she yelled 'Passengers will kindly move into the lounge as soon as they have finished'. We meekly shuffled out.

Our next ordeal was the passports. The man looked sourly at me and drawled, 'How much money have you got with you?' 'The usual', I casually replied. 'How much?', he snapped. 'Five pounds in English notes and five pounds in Swiss francs', I recited straight from the currency rules.

We moved into the Customs. When my turn came I was all prepared to say 'Nothing to declare', but a bristly man came up and said 'How much English money have you?' 'Ah- um- five pounds' (I remembered my lines). 'Exactly?' 'No- er- um- er well, £4 18s 10d'. He waved me on into a lounge which fortunately was blessed with a roaring stove. I sat down on the chair nearest to this blessing and toasted myself.

By now the time was about 7.50 a.m. and we were all looking at our watches and saying 'Not long before we're off . . .'

The engines started with a deafening roar. We taxied down the runway. 'Will you please fasten your safety belts' said the airhostess. The plane turned round and moved on to the takeoff runway. After a short wait, we began to move forward again. There was something very tense about the atmosphere in the plane. On we sped with increasing speed and I was waiting for the bump which showed we were in the air. The bump never came. I looked out of the window and saw nothing but fog. We climbed quickly and were soon above the fog and clouds. Above the clouds there seemed to be another world. Clouds rolled away on either side into valleys and hills, bumps and dips. It was very beautiful. The airhostess came round and asked me if I would like a drink. I declined. Then she came along with a plate, which I greedily accepted. On it was a wonderful assortment of snacks: turkey and ham sandwiches, crab pastries, smoked salmon on toast and sardines. They were delicious.

Katherine Whitehorn

JOURNALIST

As a small child I was always trying to keep up with my elder brother John – one of the unsung benefits of growing up is that you no longer have to prove that you can climb trees. On one occasion, he climbed up onto the parapet of a bridge over a rocky, turbulent river at Bridge of Gore in the Highlands where we always went for our summer holiday, and I climbed up after him. My mother, turning white, called to us in a strangled voice to get down, which with a bad grace we did; we were all right, the parapet was quite wide, what was all the fuss about? A friend of hers then started ticking us off for scaring her: 'How *could* you do such a thing, you *must* surely see how it would terrify your mother?' That made us feel really apologetic. Remorseful. Contrite even. We should not, of course, scare our mother. So we came back the next morning before she was up, and most considerately did it again when she couldn't see.

Bill Wiggins

When I was a child, my favourite films were films such as *The Man from Laramie* and *The Far Country*. Through this I established a deep interest in my own portrayal of the various characters I saw. I spent many of my days dressed, fully rigged out in cowboy clothes. It was at this early age that I realized my penchant for realism and detail. It was during one of frequent games when I was attempting to make everything as realistic as possible that I learned a very salutory lesson which helped me to learn exactly how fragile human life is.

My father was in the building industry and consequently had many vehicles, garages and yards in which to play. I was as usual in my cowboy outfit, with my gun slung low on my hips, with the holsters greased ready for quick action. For some reason which escapes me now, I needed fire, presumably to light the burning arrows which the Indians had. I was of course aware that petrol made it very easy to get some fire. One source of petrol was standing right beside me: a large lorry with a very large petrol tank. I proceeded to unscrew the petrol cap of this large circular petrol tank with a long funnel leading into it. I pushed a stick down the nozzle and got it soaked with petrol up to half way. Then with a match I lit the end of the stick. Immediately the wood was ablaze and I attempted to light the bonfire which I had prepared. This did not prove to be as simple as at first expected, due to using damp leaves and damp wood. I made repeated efforts to get more petrol out of the deep petrol tank. The only way was to continually use the stick and dip it into the tank. Suddenly the end of the nozzle caught fire, there was a bright glow at the top of the tube gradually creeping down to the probably fifteen or twenty gallons in the tank. I realized the danger and started to blow, this only increased the speed at which the petrol had started to burn. The harder I blew the quicker it went down the nozzle. Panic started to set in.

I realized, through of course having watched many Westerns, that explosions happened easily. What would happen once the flame hit the tank? Vivid impressions of explosions that I had seen in films came to mind. Impressions of what would happen to me if it exploded also came to mind. I blew once more using the very bottom of my lungs but the flames carried on going down. I turned and ran. I suppose I must have run perhaps forty yards when suddenly the image of my father way outshone the image of the explosion that was about to occur. It was in my mind better to be blown up in the explosion than to face the wrath of my father, who would have had half his yard, garages and vehicles destroyed. I ran back determined to do something about it. This time I stood over the nozzle convinced that the thing was going to blow up. I blew and I blew. Suddenly I put in a final desperate effort, I blew so hard that the burning petrol blew out of the nozzle into my face, singeing my hair and eyebrows, but I had succeeded in overpowering the fire. I sat down by the lorry in a state of complete shock. This, I realized, had been without doubt the closest escape of my life and I was only seven years old. This had taught me that life is very fragile and we all live day by day on an elastic band which is ready to break at any time should one make the wrong move. Needless to say, I did not report my experience to my father, I felt things were better left alone. Never did I play with fire close to petrol again.

Sir David Willcocks CBE, MC
MUSICAL DIRECTOR OF THE BACH CHOIR

When I was aged nine I joined the choir of Westminster Abbey as a probationer-chorister. I had never been away from home on my own before and I could not get to sleep during my first night at the Choir School. I lay listening to the quarterly chimes of Big Ben and soon memorized them. I find that, if asked to whistle or hum the chimes, very few of my friends (musical or otherwise) are able to do so correctly. I wonder if you, the reader of this little memoir, are one of the few who can make *no* mistakes when humming the chimes for (1) the hour, (2) the quarter, (3) the half, (4) the three-quarter. The answers are:

(1) Hour

(2) Quarter (3) Half

(4) Three-quarter

P.S. Can any reader get nearer than this (using a piano) for the 'strokes' of Big Ben?

Con. ped.

Simon Williams

ACTOR AND NOVELIST

At the age of four, in the middle of a bitterly cold snowball fight with a neighbouring girl called Judy, my mother noticed me trying some pretty underhanded trick. She called me over. 'That's not nice,' she said. 'Either you apologize to Judy or you get a smack'. I thought long and hard. At last I went over and said I was sorry. I then returned and put out my frozen hand for a smack. Come to think of it, I've never been much good at understanding the terms or conditions of a fair deal.

Bob Wilson

FORMER ARSENAL AND SCOTLAND GOALKEEPER
AND BBC PRESENTER

There was an early stage during my Junior School life when I found maths very difficult. Week after week I would receive the same mark, 0 out of 10!

Being fairly sensitive as an individual, I used to get pretty upset, sometimes tearful, at the lack of progress I was making. Unknown to me my parents went to see the teacher and explained just how disappointed I was that I wasn't able to understand the subject. They suggested that I needed to gain a little confidence and that more encouragement from the teacher would almost certainly help.

The message obviously got home because at the bottom of my next piece of work the teacher had written: '0/10. A much better effort'!

Julian Wilson
RACING COMMENTATOR

My Grandfather

My grandfather was the finest man I ever knew. His name was E.W. Mann. He was tall, with distinguished grey hair, a moustache, and an aura of greatness. Grandpa had fathered two sons and three daughters. His younger son, David, had died of tuberculosis at the age of twelve. His older son Teddy, a fine cricketer who had played for Harrow and county cricket for Kent, had been killed in the Middle East in 1942. So I, his favourite grandson, was the apple of his eye.

Grandpa had captained Harrow, Cambridge University and an M.C.C. touring side. Teddy had fulfilled his expectations. Now it was up to me.

I was known as 'Timmy' because my old nanny had once exclaimed: 'Doesn't he look a real Timothy Tudge!' Besides, in those days, Julian was a frightfully grand name for a small child.

The highlight of the day came when Grandpa would bowl to me and I to him, on the lawn before lunch. I was ten or eleven, and he was in his late sixties, but he could still turn his arm over. 'Don't try to bowl so fast, Timmy', he would complain. 'Why don't you try to spin the ball? Left-armers make far better spin-bowlers than medium pacers: and you're never going to bowl fast . . .'

One day there was a minor crisis. A next door neighbour called Simon Compton, who was at the same preparatory school as me, came up for a 'net' before lunch.

Grandpa's study had a glass frontage extending several feet from the main house wall towards the lawn. As Compton bowled I lofted my cover drive, way above the flowerbeds, hard onto the outside wall of the house. The ball ricocheted off the wall, through Grandpa's side window, into the study – and then out again through the front window! Glass was everywhere.

'You stupid boy', roared Grandpa. 'Get your foot to the ball, and keep your elbow down!'

Michael Winner MA

FILM PRODUCER, DIRECTOR AND WRITER

The Second World War was great fun. I remember being fascinated by lights in the dark. That is probably why, from a very early age, I wished to do nothing except be a film producer.

The first lights were those provided by the lamp lighter cycling along Alexander Avenue, Willesden, a street of miniature mansions, as he lit the gas lamps in the evening. I was about four at the time!

The next lights, a year later, were the traffic lights at the junction of Gloucester Terrace and I would watch them changing endlessly from my family's first floor flat. But as the war got under way there were more exciting lights to watch from that same window.

There were the searchlights that followed the air-raid warning, their beams cutting through the London darkness illuminating the anti-aircraft balloons and at times aircraft themselves. There were the explosions of shells sent aloft by the gun emplacements in Kensington Gardens which were the greatest firework display you could wish for as a youngster.

There was the reddened sky as buildings around burned. None of this seemed to present any danger to a child, it was merely an event, a happening to amuse.

Accompanying this imaginative lighting display – planes blowing up, shells exploding, searchlights, flames – were the most wonderful sounds of anti-aircraft guns, of planes droning and stopping and falling, of the warning siren and then the all-clear, meaning that the show was over.

It was of course the cheerful spirit of Londoners at that time that removed all fear from these events.

Ernie Wise OBE
COMEDIAN

When I was nine years of age my father entered me for a talent competition at a place called Morley. I won first prize, five pounds, which disappeared into my father's pocket to help the family budget. Second prize was a big 2-lb box of Black Magic chocolates. I remember thinking at the time I would rather have had the chocolates.

Terry Wogan
TELEVISION PERSONALITY

When I wasn't on my own bicycle I was on my father's.

When I was very young, he used to take me on the crossbar of that self-same bicycle and on a Sunday, as a kind of treat, we would travel together, him cycling and me sitting, to that fine purveyor of victuals to the gentry, Leverette and Frye, O'Connell Street, Limerick and I would sit among the raisins and hams while he did the book work. On the way home, he'd stop for a half-pint at Willie 'Bokkles' Gleeson's pub. Willie was called 'Bokkles', because of a small speech deficiency.

You didn't get away with much in Limerick. The merest hint of a squint, and you were known as 'boss-eyed' for the rest of your adolescent life. *Everybody* of my acquaintance had a nickname. There was 'Rogers', 'Bonk', 'Flicker', 'Mo', and I was 'Bawky'. Don't ask. I remember clearly when the leader of the gang, 'Rogers', got us all together in solemn conclave, and named us, off the top of his head. He left for Dublin with his family shortly afterwards, leaving his loyal lieutenants to battle on alone with their stigmata. Thanks a lot, Rogers.

Victoria Wood
COMEDIENNE

My very first memory is climbing out of my cot, even though it had been tied up with rope, and feeling very naughty, a feeling I still enjoy.

Childhood Memories

Michael York

ACTOR

Someone once told me that my nose was my fortune and ever
since I have often given it a curious second glance when we have
come face to face in the mirror. It's certainly not what nature
intended – whatever that was. When I was a child, I tried to fly
out of a window, with a distinct lack of success. Instead of
pulverizing my brains however, I succeeded in denting my
fledgling proboscis. It remained weak and flimsy and would
succumb to the slightest accident or ill-treatment. A minor car
crash and a fight with my sister enhanced the process, until,
as a teenager, I sported the nose I have today. Subsequent
operations to remove cartilage to ease breathing did nothing to
improve its outer shape. I strenuously resisted any subsequent
suggestions to have a 'job' done. So as a child I looked like a
young gangster – and behaved like one.

I was the leader of the pack and my headquarters was in a
cornfield in a rural hamlet just north of Oxford. War-time
shortages and deprivations meant nothing to this infant rabble-
rouser. At my command the corn was flattened into long
corridors leading into huge rooms. I ruled supreme under the
barrage balloon-filled skies. One day the law tracked me down
in my labyrinthine lair. It was a fair cop. The local constable
hauled me off home where I was berated for my lack of sense
and patriotism. I tried to go steady but to no avail. One day I hid
the embers from an illicit gangland fire at the far end of our
garden and burned down the neighbour's fence. Later I was
spotted by a sneaky train guard as I climbed out of my bedroom
window onto the roof of the house. He grassed to my commuter
father who brought me down to earth with six of the best.

As I grew up I was often mistaken for a boxer, but I scorned
this sporty association, having by now come to love the pleasures of making corridors and rooms in the groves of academy.
Even as a young actor I was mostly given 'sensitive' parts to
play. As much as I tried to vary this image with portrayals of
predatory Viking kings and 'bent' coppers, I was never quite
able to shake it off. So it was a real pleasure to be asked to play a
gangland boss in a recent film where all that early training and
suffering was gloriously vindicated and one was able to prove –
finally – that one had the nose for the part!